A portion of the proceeds from the sale of
The Great Lakes Reader will go to ABFFE,
The American Booksellers Foundation for
Free Expression.

For a searchable directory of independent bookstores
nearest you—and a list of the highly influential and
selective Indie Next Great Reads—please visit
IndieBound.org.

Visit GreatLakesReader.com to share your thoughts
and memories of your home state.

For information about *Great Lakes, Great Reads*,
the Great Lakes Booksellers Holiday Catalog,
and more, please visit www.gliba.org.

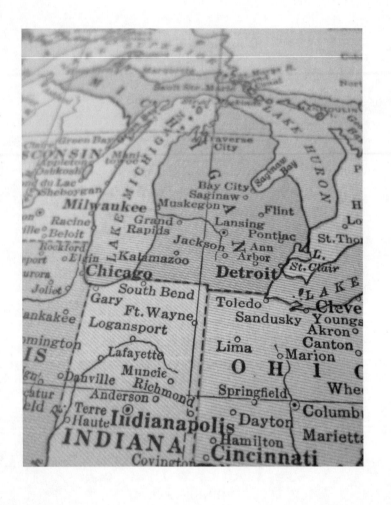

THE GREAT LAKES READER

ESSAYS ON THE STATES THAT MAKE THE **GREAT LAKES** GREAT

brought to you by
The Great Lakes Independent Booksellers Association

Edited by Carl Lennertz

DELPHINIUM BOOKS
HARRISON, NEW YORK • ENCINO, CALIFORNIA

THE GREAT LAKES READER

Printed in the United States of America.

First Edition

Designed by Greg Mortimer
Frontispiece photograph © Marisa Allegra Williams

ISBN: 978-1-883285-38-8

CONTENTS

EDITOR'S NOTE

Seventy-five years ago Franklin Delano Roosevelt put a Hall of Fame's worth of writers to work chronicling every nook and cranny of America in the famous Works Progress Administration's Federal Writers' Project. Just last year, Matt Weiland and Sean Wilsey revived the idea in a book they commissioned entitled *State by State: A Panoramic Portrait of America*, published by Ecco. It features an original essay on every state in the Union (plus Washington, D.C.) by a new generation of writers, including Dave Eggers on Illinois, Jhumpa Lahiri on Rhode Island, Ann Patchett on Tennessee, Jonathan Franzen on New York, William T. Vollmann on California, and many more.

This modern take on the WPA Guides was not meant to be exhaustive but rather highly personal, almost impressionistic—to reveal something of the essence of each state today. For instance, the essay on Missouri by NPR's Jacki Lyden focused on Bosnian immigrants bringing parts of St. Louis back to life, while the acclaimed novelist Joshua Ferris's moving piece on Florida was rooted in the sand of Key West. Thanks in no small part to the enthusiasm of independent booksellers (including a documentary produced by Powell's Books in Portland, Oregon), *State by State* was a great success throughout the country.

Inspired by the example of *State by State*, and in tribute to the extraordinary local knowledge of booksellers and librarians, we commissioned a volume devoted to the Great Lakes states written by independent booksellers and librarians themselves. These are professionals who deal with other writers' words every day of their working life, but who don't often get a chance to see their own words on paper, in a bound book, for sale in a bookstore. Some have had their work published in magazines or journals; for others, this is their debut. But all of them once lived, or still live, in the Great Lakes region and know its particularities and idiosyncrasies intimately.

Herein you will find essays on the great states of Wisconsin, Illinois, Indiana, Michigan, and Ohio, competitors in Big Ten football during the fall but comrades during the long winters, eager vacationers in the summer and hard workers year-round. Except for a hundred mile stretch on the eastern border of Ohio and a small edge of Wisconsin, these five states are completely surrounded by water—by two of our great rivers, the Ohio and Mississippi, and of course, the Great Lakes. As states they float like a unique slice of American geography and culture, but they are firmly rooted in the tradition and history of America.

We hope you enjoy these snapshots, road trips, and memories. There is love and ambivalence here, regret and happiness . . . but mostly happiness.

One final note: since I do always take the geography questions in Trivial Pursuit, I know that Minnesota, Pennsylvania and New York also touch on the Great Lakes! Look for more regional volumes written by booksellers and librarians from around the country next year; this is the first of many. Learn more at greatlakesreader.com.

Sincerely,

Carl Lennertz

ACKNOWLEDGMENTS

We'd like to thank the following groups and people:

The Great Lakes Independent Booksellers Association and the Midwest Booksellers Association, whose store member lists are in the back of this book.

Partners Book Distributor, for getting this book into bookstores quickly and efficiently.

The American Booksellers Association for their advocacy and marketing programs on behalf of independent bookstores all across the United States.

The librarians of America, who bring the joy of reading to every small town and big city in this country.

Greg Mortimer of Ecco, who donated his time to design the book cover and interior layout.

Melissa Bobotek of HarperCollins, who donated her time to copyedit the text.

Delphinium Books, an independent literary press, for funding the printing of this book, and whose three most recent books, by coincidence, are by Midwestern authors. (See the back of this book for listings and descriptions.)

And finally, to the contributors of *The Great Lakes Reader*, who donated their time and words so this book could be published in support of free speech, the rich legacies of their home states, and their fellow booksellers and librarians.

THE
GREAT
LAKES
READER

WISCONSIN

STATE NICKNAME   Badger State

STATE MOTTO   "Forward"

STATE SONG   "On, Wisconsin!"

STATE FLOWER   Wood violet

STATE DANCE   Polka

STATE ROCK   Granite

STATE SYMBOL OF PEACE   Mourning dove

STATE INSECT   Honeybee

STATE DOG   American water spaniel

RESIDENTS   Wisconsinites

STATE TRIVIA:

• The National Fresh Water Fishing Hall of Fame is housed in Hayward and is shaped like a Musky (the state fish).

• Bloomer, Wisconsin is considered the jump-rope capital of the world.

• The first Ringling Brothers Circus was staged in Baraboo in 1884.

• Famous Wisconsinites: Jackie Mason, Georgia O'Keefe, William H. Rehnquist, Orson Welles, Frank Lloyd Wright, Thornton Wilder, Gene Wilder

Life on a Wisconsin Lake

MARGIE PETERSEN WHITE

I grew up in Neenah, a small town on the shores of Lake Winnebago in northeast Wisconsin. To an outsider, that might sound idyllic, conjuring up images of picnics, sailboats, and fresh-faced ice fishermen. That's because you don't know that the name Winnebago comes from the Indian word "Ouinepegi," which means "People of Stinky Water."

The Indians were right. Every May, just in time for Mother's Day, nasty-smelling lake flies descend on the area like a biblical plague. A not-so-urban legend used to circulate around town claiming that Lake Winnebago was one of only two lakes in the entire world that produced these annoying pests—and the other was rumored to be somewhere in Siberia. Some people would actually say this boastfully.

Lake flies aren't to be confused with ordinary house flies, deer flies, horse flies, or mosquitoes, although we had plenty of those, too. Lake flies are the size of a mosquito, and though they don't bite, you almost wish they would. If so, they would attack and leave. Lake flies have no purpose; they don't even swarm. They're not that inspired. Instead, they hover in clusters like timid, mousy wallflowers at a junior high school dance.

And then they die. Together, all at the same time. In one big doozy of a Jim Jones-style mass bug suicide. I know. I've watched my folks use the extra large snow shovel to scoop up the mushy heaps of dead lake flies in the driveway. I do not say that boastfully. I say it disgustingly.

And as bad as lake flies are, that's only the half of it. By early August, Lake Winnebago manages another unique feat: it grows a world-class batch of algae. It's not like other normal lakes, which might show some green spotty growth around the edges, near the cattails or the lily pads. This stuff is thick and soupy green, whipped into a frothy, pond scummy sort of blended, fetid decaf frappuccino. Sometimes it gets so thick sea gulls can actually stand on it. It smells like a combination of dirty socks and sour milk left out in the sun for a month.

This pea soup made waterskiing on Lake Winnebago especially challenging. Because it was such a big lake, it was often choppy with whitecaps. If you wanted to ski, you either had to wait for the wind to calm down, or you had to steer your boat toward all the sheltered alcoves and bays. Unfortunately, that's where the pea soup was, and it took a lot of confidence to ski through it. Most people are afraid of falling, so they hang onto the ski rope with a death grip.

My brother and I, on the other hand, considered it an extra thrill to ski right through it and watch our legs turn green. Or better yet, pull a really tight slalom turn and throw up a huge wall of green spray. Sometimes the wind brought the wall of pea soup right back into your face, and you were left spitting and sputtering, wiping green goo from your eyes so you could see the half-gagging, half-admiring looks from the passengers on the boat. We had to come home and soak our green-stained swimsuits in the sink.

Many years later, I learned that our lovely pea soup was caused in part by something environmentalists call "nutrients." My brother, now a college professor with a knack for translating complicated scientific terminology into actual English, explains that "nutrients" is just a nice way of saying "poop." The old lake cottages had poor or no sewage systems, resulting in run-off into the lake. Additionally, because Lake Winnebago is located right smack in the heart of The Dairy State, its nutrients had an extra ingredient: cow poop. The cows frequently go right up to the water for a drink (and whatever else cows do).

My brother and I used to enjoy terrorizing the local cow population when we were waterskiing. If you got close enough to a herd of cows drinking at the water's edge, you could soak them with a nice, big slalom spray. Once, I caused a small stampede, and cows scrambled and piled on top of each other to climb a muddy hill to safety. My brother and I couldn't stop snickering that the cows' milk would be sour for several days from the fright, leaving their farmer completely puzzled. Now that's Wisconsin humor for you.

Despite all the scientific evidence supporting the nutrient explanation, Lake Winnebago natives continue to prefer (again, rather proudly) the "two lakes in the whole world" theory. Something at the bottom of our lake and that of our Siberian sister lake encourages the growth of lake flies in May, the deluge of algae in August, and one more strange and local phenomenon: the survival of the sturgeon.

Sturgeon are a relatively rare, prehistoric-looking fish. They have bony plates instead of scales and actually lived in the time of the dinosaurs. I remember them as butt-ugly, bottom-sucking, whiskered beasts that had a lead role in my childhood nightmares, right along with the hot-breath bear. Some sturgeons are bigger than humans, growing up to twelve feet long. This is especially creepy to think about in a lake that is usually less than twelve feet deep. I imagined them floating like malevolent mermaids in an upright, tail-down position, able to pluck their lunch right off the surface. My mother tried to calm me by telling me that they didn't have teeth. That "they were more afraid of me than I was of them." But of course she said that about bears, too.

Sturgeon are amazing creatures. They can live to be 150 years old, and I've heard the record-setting sturgeon caught in Lake Winnebago weighed 182 pounds. Winnebago Indians revered them, and the Menominee tribe included them in their creation myth. For some reason, Lake Winnebago contains the largest self-sustaining population of lake sturgeon in the world. Experts currently estimate that there are nearly 50,000 sturgeon in Lake Winnebago alone. I'm not good at math, but doesn't that mean there are approximately 230 sturgeons per square mile? Some things you would just rather not know. I don't think they brag about that in the Winnebago County real-estate brochures.

Unlike lake flies and pea soup, there is an interesting flipside to the sturgeon problem of Lake Winnebago: caviar. Talk about two things that just don't go together: Gatsby-like aristocrats sipping martinis and nibbling on exquisite caviar, versus Wisconsin ice fisherman with Day-Glo orange snowmobile suits, sucking down a case of Old Milwaukee, dragging their speared, egg-laden female sturgeon up into their Lake Winnebago shanties.

Wisconsin men are proud of their ice shanties. They're a combination of tree fort, playhouse, igloo and sports bar. Some even have electricity, either from power generators or electrical cords dangerously stretched over football fields of frozen tundra. The electricity isn't needed to keep the beer cool, but rather to keep the Packers game on—and the microwave and hotplate. Some shanties have wallpaper, some have cute little gingham curtains. The object is to sit there, look down the hole, wait for a sturgeon to swim by, and watch a football game.

My dad actually caught a sturgeon once. It was a female, and as they like to say, he harvested the eggs. Saying it that way makes me think of in vitro fertilization, but I can assure you, the extraction was neither delicate nor antiseptic. It's kind of like gutting a deer, which is yet another slice of life in Wisconsin. The funny thing about sturgeon fishing is that after all that trouble, and in spite of the luxurious reputation of caviar, it's against Wisconsin law to sell the eggs. Locals insist Lake Winnebago caviar is superior to Beluga caviar from the Caspian Sea, and claim they could get at least $500 for a belly-full of eggs on the black market—in theory. Not that the good, mostly honest fishermen of Lake Winnebago would do that kind of thing.

You're probably wondering why anyone would ever want to live near a poopy green lake that's filled to the brim with dead lake flies and prehistoric monster fish. In our know-it-all, I'm-outta-here days of early adulthood, my brother and I used to laugh at the bumper stickers that said "Escape to Wisconsin"—shouldn't they say "Escape *from* Wisconsin?" We quickly ditched our Fargo-like "hey, dare" accents for post-grad school metropolitan coolness.

So why, over thirty years later, is there a big red Wisconsin Badger flag hanging from my front porch? Why would I send my daughter to the University of Wisconsin—Madison, where the orientation advisor admitted that some of the boys use their dorm room refrigerators to store venison in deer hunting season? Because the truth is, in spite of everything, I've become the bumper sticker I used to make fun of. I really do ♥ Wisconsin.

I loved growing up on Lake Winnebago. I spent most of my summers in it, on it, or near it. As a toddler, I took my best naps under the highly varnished deck of our family's 1960 white Oconto Cruiser, lined with pillows and stuffed animals. On sleepless middle-aged nights, I would give anything to feel that drugged, drooling sensation of being under that deck, my tummy full of Kool-Aid and peanut butter and jelly sandwiches, fading in and out of sleep, listening to the water sloshing against the sides of the boat.

As a young girl, I could bring along a new Nancy Drew book and go on day-long boat rides without ever getting bored, my pigtails flapping in the breeze like a dog with its head out the car window. As I got older, the books may have changed—from *The Happy Hollisters* and *Pippi Longstocking* to *Elizabeth Bennett* and *Jane Eyre*—but the rides didn't. The best thing about boat rides, especially as a teen, was the way you could combine reading and tanning without breaking a sweat. (This was back in the day before sunscreen had numbers, when we thought baby oil, iodine and tinfoil was a nifty idea.) We came home looking like lobsters, our skin simmering with radiation. Today, I still love a good book on a boat ride, but my dermatologist insists on SPF 50.

Boat rides in Wisconsin can go on forever. I don't know why Minnesota gets all the credit for being the Land of Ten Thousand Lakes, and Wisconsin got tagged as the Dairy State. Wisconsin has tons of lakes, plus it has an added bonus: many of them are chains of lakes. It even has a town up north called Chain O' Lakes. Anyway, from Lake Winnebago, you could reach a whole new series of lakes and connecting tributaries, from Big and Little Lake Butte des Morts (Do other states do that, too? The whole big and little lake thing?) to the Wolf River, over miles and miles of hairpin turns around sandy little beaches. Of course, we did this back when gas was about nineteen cents a gallon.

Our boat rides started every Sunday as soon as church got out. Actually, a little bit before. My mother, an early-adopter cafeteria Catholic, thought it was perfectly okay to sneak out of mass early. You go up to the altar, receive communion, and then very nonchalantly ditch out the side door. (She also thought it balanced things out a little better if she matched her donations to the church with contributions to the National Organization for Women. Something to note: Wisconsin women have long had minds of their own.) We hurried home to pack the cooler with enormous quantities of bologna sandwiches and grape pop, get the boat ready, and be on our way. My mom used to say she could appreciate the gifts of God more out on the boat with her family than in a stuffy old church.

On any given Sunday, we might boat east across the lake to hike through poison ivy at High Cliff State Park, or head up to Waverly Beach, where we would anchor the boat and spend hours hopping in ocean-sized waves. Whatever happened to all those old-fashioned inner tubes from the car dealer? Big, black, sturdy and (best of all) recycled before recycling was cool. They absorbed the heat from the sun and became your own personal bun warmer. So much better than those flimsy little pink plastic tubes from Wal-Mart that you buy one day and throw away the next.

Every summer, we took the boat down to Oshkosh to watch the EAA Air Show from the lake. It was a great way to avoid the heat and the crowds on the grounds of the airport. The planes would fly right over our heads on their circular route back to the show. I loved it when my dad taught me to identify the different World War II planes, from a P-51 Mustang to the B-17 Flying Fortress. He knew them all from his tour of duty in the Philippines.

My dad said once that he thought it was our boat rides that kept our family together. I didn't get it at the time. True understanding would have to wait until I had teenagers of my own, when I too would suffer that peculiar sense of loss and nostalgia. That weird push-and-pull inside a family getting older together. Our boat rides were our family time. My brother and I joined willingly, eagerly, innocently. As if we weren't embarrassed by our parents on land.

Having a boat made us feel lucky. My dad was a millworker with a lunch bucket; we lived a good and simple life. Our boat was our extravagance and the lake was our escape. I remember our sense of good fortune as we motored along the shore of Riverside Park, past hot, uncomfortable families spread out on blankets in the shade. We couldn't believe our luck—we had a boat! We could go out to the middle of the lake where the breeze was strong and the water was cool and clean. Never mind that our boat was just a small one; it never even registered that there were others much luckier than we were, cruising by in their glamorous sailboats or nearly swamping us with the wake from their giant multi-decked cabin cruisers.

Our sense of being lucky on the lake sustained us in difficult times. One very sad summer, my mother spent her last days of life floating on the lake. She had a brain tumor, and by the time August came, she could barely walk or speak. My dad would lift her into her floating chaise lounge, complete with cup holders in each armrest, and she would spend hours being rocked gently by the waves. The days were gloriously hot and dry and sunny, the kind of days you would want if you had only a few left on earth. The lake was perfectly behaved, it was deliciously warm, and the waves were neither too big nor too small. I don't remember any pea soup that August at all. At the end of each of these last days, my mother would exclaim with utterly pure gratitude: "That was another 'triple A' day!" The lake took care of her and we were thankful. Later, we would trust the lake to cradle my mother's ashes in its warm, sweet embrace.

It's not often that I get back to Lake Winnebago anymore. I left Wisconsin decades ago. My dad is still there, but he lives on a different lake in Waupaca now. It's a pretty, shimmering, glacier-fed lake: there are no algae, no lake flies, and no sturgeon. Just cute little bass, bluegills and sunfish. It's a safe, small, calm lake, perfect for an eighty-year-old to putt-putt around in on a pontoon boat. "Waupaca" comes from the Indian words for "land of golden waters." That's got to beat the "land of stinky water" any day. But there's also no history for me, no memories, no deep connection to every summer of my childhood.

Just one footnote though. My stepmother swears that there is a large, lone sturgeon residing in the depths of Miner Lake on the Waupaca Chain of Lakes. She and her daughter have both seen it. They're Lake Winnebago natives, so I really shouldn't doubt them. Tourists on pontoon boats have reportedly spotted it, gotten all excited, and screamed "Shark!" (They're probably from Illinois. Wisconsin joke.) I'm still in denial over these sightings, probably because it upsets my satisfying dichotomy: Lake Winnebago vs. Miner Lake; past vs. present. On the other hand, a single sturgeon in the land of golden waters makes a perfect metaphor—it's a reminder that the past is always with you. Most of the time it's down too deep to notice; it only surfaces now and then. But as both my mother and my stepmother would say, "Don't worry, it won't hurt you."

Looking back, I now understand why the Indians from Lake Winnebago named themselves The People of the Stinky Water. First of all, it's always better to make fun of yourself before somebody else does. Modern-day Packers fans definitely get this with all of their good-natured cheesehead gear. But more than that, I think the Indians embraced the name out of a great and deep wisdom. With a sense of wonder and luck, of gratitude and defiance, with humility and reverence toward the laws of nature. With respect, not fear, for the past, and appreciation for the history of their ancestors. It was their announcement to the world: "Sure it's stinky, but so what? It's our home and we really do ♥ Wisconsin."

• • •

Margie Petersen White was born and raised in Wisconsin, and has spent most of her adult life in the neighboring state of Illinois. She is a part-time litigation attorney and a bookseller at The Bookstore in Glen Ellyn, a suburb of Chicago.

The Many Sides of Wisconsin

KIRK FARBER

America's Dairyland. The Badger State. Home of the Green Bay Packers. Domain of the cheeseheads.

My first realization that I lived in a state named Wisconsin occurred before I entered grade school. My dad was a traveling bookseller for Follett Publishing, and his territory covered grade schools in all seventy-two counties. He sold social-studies textbooks, and our garage always had stacks of them lining the walls.

My mother and sister and I served as his audience while he practiced his slideshow presentations. We learned how the explorer Jean Nicolet founded the Green Bay Colony, and how French fur traders continued to settle the area until Britain took over. We learned that Wisconsin officially became the thirtieth U.S. state in 1848, that its official bird is the robin, and its slogan is "Forward!" But because history is not that interesting to a five-year old, there was really only one fact about Wisconsin I held in high regard as a child: Wisconsin is shaped like an enormous kid's mitten, the hand closed against the cold.

Geographically, the state is made up of several distinct sections. Most of my experiences living in Wisconsin were focused in the territories I like to unofficially call: Greater Farmland, Northwoods, and Milwaukee. Greater Farmland is largely the southern half of the state where all the farmin' happens: corn, soybeans, and cows. The Northwoods is the northern third of the state, covered in pine trees, which also borders chilly Lake Superior. And Milwaukee, while technically resting in the southeast corner of Greater Farmland, is the state's largest city, and really, a world away from the rest of Wisconsin.

GREATER FARMLAND

If you drive into Wisconsin from Illinois on I-94, one of the first roadside attractions you will encounter is the Mars Cheese Castle. Giant yellow letters proclaim the castle's name in neon, and medieval flags jut skyward to draw your attention, in case you missed the afore-mentioned massive neon cheese sign.

I love driving by this place because like many Wisconsinites, it is unashamed of what it is. In this case, it's a building full of cheese, a portal to America's Dairy-land. A cheese castle. While this may seem a little, well, cheesy—isn't that the point? Have you ever tried cheese curds? They squeak when you eat them. What other foods squeak when you eat them? This is cause for celebration.

My little hometown is named Oconomowoc, pro-nounced Oh-KHAN-oh-moe-wok. Sure, it's tough to say, but it's still easier than Faulkner's Yoknapatawpha County. With a population of just over 12,000, Oconomowoc rests in the middle of Greater Farmland, near other cities with Native American names like Wauke-sha and Pewaukee and Chenequa. Also nestled amongst several lakes, this town was a great place to be a kid in. If you were wealthy, you lived on a lake and you were known as a "lakie." If you were not wealthy, you tried to find friends who were. Or, you did what I did and went fishing with your dad after he was done selling books. Or, you rode your bike to the gravel pit reservoir, dug deep by cement companies in search of rock. Affectionately known as "The Pit," this edge-of-the-suburbs playground had hundred-foot-tall piles of rocks to climb and jump off, and bottomless mini-lakes that were excellent for swimming and bass fishing but a source of constant worry for parents. Over time, the narrow quarry grew wider with extended excavation until several of the ponds were merged to form as one large body of water. Today, the dirt bike paths of my youth have been paved with streets, and the shores of "The Pit" have been repackaged and sold as luxury homes on "Crystal Lake." I guess you really can't go home again.

The smells can be strong in Greater Farmland. The putrid pig manure sprayed on crops mix with spring's blooms of lilacs and honeysuckle. Fall brings the crispy sun-baked scent of autumn leaves. As a kid, the smell of soil and cornstalks was a daily intake as I ran through rows of six-foot plants on my way home from school.

A Norman Rockwell quality seeps through the small towns of Greater Farmland—a feeling of simpler times. You see gazebos and boutique shops, ball parks and parades. This makes it a fun place to be a kid or raise a family, but as a teenager, life can be torturously boring. My friends and I often reached a dead-end in our search for entertainment during adolescence. The cool kids in small-town Wisconsin met in secret fields and had kegger parties with bonfires and loud music. The geeky bandheads (that's me) stayed home and watched movies and wondered what the cool kids were doing.

I've seen the cow-tipping stunt in many movies—bored teenagers sneaking up on a helpless bovine so they can push it over while it sleeps—but I've never seen it live, nor have I known anyone to partake in such an activity. In fact, I think it all might be a myth. Besides, you don't tip cows in America's Dairyland. It's disrespectful.

Wisconsin's dairy industry generates over $20 billion a year for the state's economy. 14,000 operations care for 1.25 million dairy cows. And they're not just cows; they're Holsteins and Guernseys and Milking Shorthorns.

Even with all the new technology, farming is hard work, definitely not for the faint-of-heart. And if you're not used to the hard realities of farm talk, it can be a little jarring. Last Thanksgiving, my wife's uncle told us a farming story over dinner. It was about his live-stock, and he started it like this: "There I was, shoulder deep in asshole."

The weather is of prime importance to farmers and non-farmers alike. And while not always favorable, Wisconsin's forecasts are not complicated. It is hot and humid and overcast in the summer. It is frigid and snowy and overcast in the winter. In between these seasons are fleeting days sometimes referred to as "spring "and "fall." Catch them if you can. The week of autumn can be stunning if the leaves change to bright oranges and reds. Or it can be wet and miserable and vaguely yellow-green.

My wife, Kelly, and I were married in the farmland town of Oshkosh, in a June outdoor ceremony that now seems to defy logic. Why we chose to brave the odds of Wisconsin weather, I'm not sure. And how we ended up with a sunny, warm, and dry day, I will never know. We just thanked our lucky stars, and headed to our mini-honeymoon destination, a place where many had gone before us: Up North.

NORTHWOODS

In Wisconsin, if someone tells you they are going "up north" for vacation, that is all that needs to be said. This means not Greater Farmland and not Milwaukee.

Actually mentioning cities like Rice Lake or Cable or Minocqua is unnecessary. You are just going up north: majestic forests, streams, and lakes await. There will be mosquitoes also. Big ones. Traveling in swarms.

The gateway to Up North is the destination city of Wisconsin Dells, about one hour north of Madison. This is where the dark, pungent farmland suddenly shifts to fragrant pine trees. The air feels lighter, and the sky seems to take on a different hue.

Wisconsin Dells is also where you'll find more waterslides than anywhere else on the planet, and why it is known as the Waterpark Capital of the World. Throughout the town are all manner of twisting, brightly colored plastic tubes—snaking in and out of the walls of hotels, undulating up and down hills, propped up on elaborate support systems. You will see giant wave pools and surfing simulators, speed slides and piles of inner tubes. This is Wisconsin's Disneyland, and families flock here.

In the summer, the Dells can be a noisy place. Helicopter tours fly overhead. The Ducks—an armada of leftover amphibious Army vehicles—groan through town before they splash straight into the river and continue their tours afloat. And until Lake Delton was recently drained into the river leaving a giant hole where a lake used to be, Tommy Bartlett would entertain thousands with his waterskiing shows à la The Go-Go's "Vacation" video.

The downtown is lined with souvenir shops full of beaded moccasins and glass trinkets, wolf paintings and T-shirts. For a kid, Wisconsin Dells is a dream destination: junk toys and ice cream and fudge and water rides. What more could there possibly be in life?

My family frequented Hayward, near the top of the state. And we went fishing, because that's what you do in a city that is home to the world's largest fiberglass sculpture in the shape of a fish. At four- and-a-half stories tall, the giant muskellunge is also part of the National Freshwater Fishing Hall of Fame. This is where you take photos of yourself catching impossibly large bluegill and browse the halls to see world record catches, tackle box panoramas, and minnow box showcases.

Afterwards, you take your boat on Lake Chippewa, and find a back bay with a nice drop-off. You toss out a Mepps bucktailed Musky Killer, start cranking, and watch the spoon flashing the dark water. You hope that you will catch a record yourself, preferably one of those monsters that are rumored to be so big it will eat your toes if you dangle them in the water, or that are capable of sucking a duckling, whole, right off the surface.

Most of the time, the fish are too smart. Most of the time, the statisticians are right that it takes 10,000 casts to catch one musky. But you never know if you don't have your line in the water, so you keep casting, and you keep cranking that reel, and you listen to the soundtrack of the loons as they sing their spooky song in the distance.

Northwoods culture would be incomplete without mentioning hunting. Bow season. Rifle season. Turkey, duck, bear. And the granddaddy of them all: deer hunting.

Wisconsin is known as one of the nation's premier deer hunting states. For nine days, thousands of hunters find their way to the Northwoods, armed with rifles and dressed in blaze orange. Out of the thriving herd of over 1.5 million deer, the hunters take home about 300,000 during one season—also known as "the harvest."

I've never been deer hunting, but I remember portions of my eighth-grade class disappearing en masse during the season—a third of all male students vanishing as if by some terrible plague. Suddenly gym class was strangely quiet, and the teachers were slightly more relaxed due to the decrease in population. But then, just as quickly, they returned, with stories of the hunt—how snow fell this year and allowed them to track the white-tails, how eight-point bucks were strapped to pickups, and how at that moment a gutted carcass was hanging from the rafters in their garage.

Our neighbor, Buster, would bring over stacks of venison steaks in a good year, happy and proud to share his abundance. "Take as much as you like, we'll never eat it all," he told us, but he warned us about the taste. "It's a little gamey."

MILWAUKEE

Out of the woods and into the city, you'll find Milwaukee, the largest urban place in the state. The population is large enough to offer big-city amenities but small enough to be family-friendly. There are several universities, some of the best hospitals in the country, and a major league baseball team named the Brewers—as Milwaukee has been home to several of America's largest breweries.

The city rests on the shores of the great Lake Michigan, and its Lake Park was designed by the same man who designed New York City's Central Park, Frederick Law Olmsted. Another world-renowned architect, Santiago Calatrava, designed a new art museum that sits on the lake's edge, looking like some sort of modern bird-ship complete with retractable wings. Nearby is an enviable marina.

And yet Milwaukeeans have a tendency to be self-deprecating. It's a quality that reaches beyond the city, a charming humility perhaps born of a working class mentality. People generally tend to avoid drawing attention to themselves, and eschew all things pretentious—they might eschew the word *eschew*.

Part of this self-esteem problem might be due to the fact that only ninety miles to the south lies the sprawling metropolis of Chicago. With a population of 600,000, Milwaukee can hardly compete with Chicago's three million. There is no Sears Tower in Milwaukee. There is no Oprah.

Now that I live out of the state, I can take it upon myself to do a little boasting and say this: Milwaukee has a few things on Chicago. It's much more accessible, it's easier to navigate, and it has an impressive variety of restaurants. And Milwaukee kicks ass when it comes to festivals, which is probably how it came to be known as the City of Festivals.

In a given year, you can drive down to the lakefront and attend African World Festival, Arab Fest, Asian Fest, Bastille Days, Festa Italiana, German Fest, Indian Summer, Irish Fest, Mexican Fiesta, Polish Fest, and Pride Fest. Milwaukee knows how to celebrate its diversity.

The most grandiose of all the festivals, however, is Summerfest—the world's largest outdoor music festival. When I lived in town, I always had a love-hate relationship with this one. You've got to love knowing that for eleven days, you have access to a steady stream of A-list performers, breezy lake weather, an endless amount of food from a variety of cultures, and Brewtown beer. But like any resident in a town that has a tourist attraction, you can begin to resent the influx of visitors—the 100,000 people who clog the highways nightly, honking their horns, whooping out their car windows. It's like a rock concert times one hundred for over a week. By the end, you're ready to get your quiet little city back.

Whether it's the festivals of Milwaukee, the fishing of the Northwoods, or the simplicity of Greater Farmland, the people are really the stars of Wisconsin. There is a certain vibe you get from Wisconsinites that is hard to pin down. To be sure, they are friendly, humble, good-natured folks who put an emphasis on family and friends and community. Not that these qualities don't exist in other places, but you get a heaping helping of it in Wisconsin.

I remember my dad returning from his book sales trips, after spending days on the road presenting to teachers and librarians all over the state. He always had stories to share about those trips—the busyness of Milwaukeeans, the quiet humor of farm town residents, the slight shift in dialect as you drive further north. He enjoyed traveling around Wisconsin. Tourists may not arrive in droves to marvel at America's Dairyland, or flock there for a sunny retirement, but the people who live there find it hard to leave.

• • •

Kirk Farber now lives with his wife in Colorado, and works in a library with a view of the mountains. His debut novel, *Postcards from a Dead Girl*, will be published by HarperPerennial in March 2010.

ILLINOIS

STATE NICKNAME Prairie State

STATE TREE White oak

STATE GRASS Big bluestem

STATE BIRD Cardinal

STATE ANIMAL White-tailed deer

STATE INSECT Monarch butterfly

STATE DANCE Square dancing

STATE FOSSIL Tully monster

OFFICIAL SNACK FOOD Popcorn

RESIDENTS Illinoisans

STATE TRIVIA:

• The world's first skyscraper, the ten-story Home Insurance Building, was built in Chicago in 1885.

• Metropolis, the home of Superman, actually exists in southern Illinois.

• Illinois boasts the largest number of personalized license plates in the U.S.

• Famous Illinoisans: Jack Benny, Ray Bradbury, Raymond Chandler, Miles Davis, Walt Disney, Benny Goodman, Charlton Heston, Quincy Jones, Abraham Lincoln, David Mamet, Bob Newhart, Bill Murray, Ronald Reagan, Carl Sandburg, Oprah Winfrey

Hunt for Illinois

JOSH K. STEVENS

I've spent my entire young life in Illinois, but it dawned on me recently that I really know nothing about the state that I live in.

I shouldn't say I know *nothing* about the twenty-first state of the Union. I know that this is the Land of Lincoln. Even though he wasn't born here, he did spend forty-eight famous years here. I know that we grow a lot of corn, running second in the national production of those little yellow kernels in 2004. I know that the capital is Springfield and that we're bordered, going counterclockwise, by the great states of Wisconsin, Iowa, Missouri, Kentucky, and Indiana, and that much of our border is liquid, with the Mississippi River to the west, the Ohio River on the south, and that great inland sea, Lake Michigan, to the east. Granted, that's all great knowledge to have, but I really should know more than those few bits of trivia about my home.

When I was a kid, my family took a lot of road-trip vacations. I remember that, when people would ask me where I was from, I always started out by saying St. Charles (where we lived until I was twelve) and, after countless polite head nods that told me that people had no idea where I was talking about, I would wind up just being vague and telling people I was from Illinois. The same thing happened when we moved to Woodstock. I figured that a new hometown would garner a new response. I was wrong. However, it was at this point that I realized that I could just tell people that I was from Chicago because, after all, Woodstock was only an hour outside of the Windy City.

That did it. Once I started saying I was from Chicago, I started getting better responses. The name alone had notoriety. The mention of Chicago came with connotations of dirty politicians, the untouchables, gangsters, mobsters, the outfit, Al Capone, and John Dillinger. It also came with images of other things (the blues, John Hughes movies, etc.), but those things didn't garner my favorite reaction which I received from a Chinese man running a hot dog stand in Florida when I was fifteen:

"Where you from, kid?"

"Chicago."

"Ohhh, Chicago. Bang, bang!"

But while telling people I was from the City of Big Shoulders kept things interesting, it was a blatant lie. Back then, I couldn't have told anyone what El train would take them to Wrigley field, nor could I have told them the difference between Clark Street and Michigan Avenue. That is the same problem I have with Illinois. I am from the town of Woodstock in McHenry County and our claim to fame was "The Birthplace of Dick Tracy" until last summer, and is now "Groundhog Day was filmed here." I'm serious. The movie was filmed in 1992 and we still have a citywide celebration of it every year that people come from all over the United States to partake in. If you ask me about Woodstock and McHenry County, I can answer your questions; about Illinois, not so much.

It's been eleven years since my run in with the "bang, bang" hot dog guy and now I live in a studio apartment on the Historic Woodstock Square, a picturesque postcard of a town, with cobblestone streets, beautiful old buildings, and a lush green park with a gazebo in the center. My apartment is one block away from my full-time job at our local independent bookstore, and just short of a block away from my part-time job at the Woodstock Opera House.

I haven't been outside of Illinois for more than two days in the last decade and I actually go days on end without ever leaving a three-block radius of my apartment. My commute to work doesn't even give me enough time to smoke a cigarette and my treks to a local bar rarely take me five feet from my front door. I shop at a local convenience store that I can literally see from my apartment and I regularly frequent the dozen local eateries that are a five-minute walk from my place. One would assume that I have a nice little eco-sphere going for me.

And I mostly do. Don't get me wrong; I love Woodstock. I love the hometown feel, I love the way it looks, I love that everyone knows me. For the most part. The trouble in paradise is that I feel a bit like George Bailey. I could walk around Woodstock like Jimmy Stewart with a smile plastered on my face, telling the movie theater and the old savings and loan how much I love them, but it doesn't change the fact that I feel as though I've missed out on seeing the world.

I've often dreamed about taking a couple weeks off and going on my own trip across the country, seeing places that I've seen or read about in movies, books, and magazines. I imagine myself hopping into a car with the drunken spirit of Jack Kerouac, the drug-addled ghost of Hunter S. Thompson, and the safe anchoring mirage of George Bailey, revving up the engine and setting off down Route 66 on a road trip that would put all other road trips to shame. But too often, I just can't come up with the time or the money or a combination of both to join them, so I'm left in the dust as they drive off, saying "Maybe next year." It's my own fault, not the fault of Donna Reed's amazing smile or my absent-minded uncle misplacing the payroll. Regardless, I remain in Woodstock, year after year, watching the days go by. At twenty-six, I'm already stuck in my own routine and time certainly isn't slowing down. In fact, it seems to be accelerating.

On Valentine's Day, I got off work earlier than usual and Arlene, my boss, suggested that, rather than sitting around my apartment being miserable, I should go for a drive. I was non-committal, but the thought played in my mind on that absurdly short trip home. As soon as I got there, I pulled out a three-year old road atlas that

I'd never used and flipped through to Illinois. I stared at the map for a while, thinking about how little of my home state I had really seen. Even on family vacations, which were generally spent in the backseat of the car passing the time reading, sleeping, or fighting with my sister, I could remember very little of the sights we had passed on our way to other destinations. I decided, then and there, that I would heed Arlene's advice and take that drive. I grabbed a handful of CDs and headed out the door to my car, ready to become one with the open road—at least for the day.

I had no destination in mind, save for heading West. East was familiar suburbs, then Chicago, which I have come to know and love. West was something new. Something different.nI conjured up an image of the mighty Mississippi, the beast that it is thanks to good old Mark Twain. I knew that you had to cross that old river to get through the plains to the mountains, then to the desert and, finally, to the Pacific Ocean in all its glory. Granted, I wasn't going that far, not today, but you have to walk before you run, and the Mississippi River was a good step. Even if it was just to cross over to another state to look back on my own.

I had barely been on the road for fifteen minutes

before I became a little antsy. The car ahead of me was moving far too slow and the cornfields didn't exactly provide the dramatic change in vista I was looking for. Besides, I had driven this road before. Far too many times. I turned off on a backroad, which would lead me to the road I needed to be on to reach the Mississippi. It did make me feel alive to be cruising down the highway, shedding my George Bailey skin for the day and knowing that there was no possible way that I would run into someone I knew from home. That was a problem for me in Woodstock. Just like Jimmy Stewart, everyone knew who I was. I couldn't walk to the end of my block without having ten conversations with ten different people. The majority of the time, that was all well and good. Normally I didn't mind, but there were other times when it would be nice to be anonymous., such as when I was on a date.

As I came to a stoplight, it dawned on me that I was at a familiar crossroads. And not a metaphorical one; a real one. If I turned right, I would be at my ex-girlfriend's house, and if I turned left, I would find my way to my grandparents. I was still in the gravitational pull of Woodstock.

I wondered if that was what Illinois was all about for

me. Perhaps no matter where I journeyed in the state, I would always be somewhere where someone knew me. Maybe there was just no place to hide in the Land of Lincoln. Maybe I was always going to be just six degrees away from someone familiar. Even in Chicago, which is a state of its own in a way, home to 2,896,016 people, I bet I could round a corner coming out of a pub and run into someone that I dated or once worked with. But that's the dichotomy of small-town Illinois, or small town U.S.A., for that matter—the simultaneous comfort and claustrophobia of other people. You can't pick and choose your interactions based on the mood you're in. You just have to go out there and deal with it. I suppose that the alternative—no one stopping to chat, no one saying hello, no one caring—would be worse.

When the light turned green I turned up the volume on the Tom Petty CD and shot ahead, eager to break out of the orbit known as home, even with the endless galaxy of cornfields spreading out around me. But it'd be awhile. Each mile I passed was pretty much the same as the last; just cows and corn and barns. It was either farmland or, as I approached a town or city via the major highways, strip malls built on what used to be farmlands.

I shouldn't make it sound as though Illinois is like this everywhere. I haven't really traveled into the southern section of the state. I know that there are pieces of divergent flair hidden among the state's cornstalks, notably in its university towns. As I recall, Springfield has a great deal of historical value. Most notably a giant, shiny decapitated head of Abraham Lincoln that brings good luck to anyone who rubs his nose. Maybe this is more bizarre than historical, but it's different all the same. Still, apart from that, there are a lot of cornfields.

Halfway to the Mississippi, the Rock River runs north-south, acting as something of a warm-up river for my journey. When I crossed over the Rock River and into Oregon, Illinois, I was pleased at the breath of fresh air that it brought. It was different from the other towns I had passed through. It was quaint and picturesque, filled with historic buildings, Mom-and-Pop shops, pleasant-looking people, and cobblestone streets. I was tempted to end my travels there and eat at a diner overlooking the river and some beautiful bluffs, but it hit me that, minus the bluffs and the river, I had just described Woodstock. I opted to continue on my way. I didn't want to feel comfortable because things felt familiar. I wanted to feel something new and different. I wanted to find someplace that would have the same effect on me as when Dorothy went from black-and-white to color. What exactly that was had yet to be determined, but I was hell-bent on finding it.

So I drove on, hoping to reach the Mississippi River by sunset, and I was glad that I did; the landscape finally began to change. The farmland gave way to some hills. I could no longer see the horizon. As I traveled on, the hills got larger and more rolling, almost creating a mountainous feel (a term I use loosely, considering that the highest point in Illinois is 1,235 feet above sea level). I passed the Land of Oz Food Court, Craft & Antique Mall, Gas Station, and Subway Sandwich Shop. I wanted to stop, if only to see if I could get a T-shirt, but it was getting late.

The sun was already getting dangerously close to the hills as I crested a bluff overlooking the town of Savanna. I drove down the main drag, which was surprisingly quiet for a Saturday night Valentine's Day. If I had more than the twenty dollars in my pocket (some planner, this guy), I probably would've stopped in at one of the many bars along the road, which were homely but welcoming. I had slowed down to take a closer look at one of the bars, still contemplating stopping in for a brew, when I caught a glimpse of the raging river. My goal was within spitting distance and the sun had yet to go down. I turned a corner and found myself on a steel bridge. I felt giddy, like an ancient nomad finding his way to the Promised Land. I looked at the mighty river stretching out beneath me. I passed over the bridge and found myself, still overjoyed, on a narrow stretch of road surrounded by the river. Then I saw the sign off to the side of the road, standing proud. WELCOME TO IOWA.

I drove through the tiny town of Sabula (which, I would find out later, is the only island in the state of Iowa). I followed the road to an outcrop, where I stopped and stepped out of my car. I was on an island in the middle of the Mississippi River. Take that, Huck Finn. I stood in silence, smoking my cigarette and watching the sun set slowly in the west. When the sun had disappeared behind the bluffs, I turned back around, facing east, and took in Illinois in all its glory. I realized, looking at my state from a new perspective, that no matter how boring Illinois seemed to me while I was standing within the confines of her borders, the state would always be my home. All of my memories, all of my friends and family, everything I knew and loved—it was all in Illinois. No matter what happened or where life lead me from this point forward, I would always be a part of Illinois and she would always be a part of me, just as Bedford Falls was to George Bailey. It was actually kind of comforting. Maybe a spontaneous road trip had been the way to getting out of a rut. Not only had it taken my mind off the miserable holiday that is Valentine's Day, it had also allowed me to get to know Illinois a little better.

I'll admit, though, that getting back in the car was the hardest part of the trip. I had to force myself not to keep heading west to see what the rest of the country had to offer. I made myself turn around and start on my trip home. One day, I'll take that ride and see the country from the driver's seat of adulthood and not the back seat of my youth. Arms outstretched, windows down, music on, the trusty atlas by my side, I'd find more Woodstocks, Chicagos, and everything in between, and after I accomplish that, I know that Illinois will welcome me back with open arms.

• • •

Josh K. Stevens's short stories have been published in RAGAD, Boston Literary Magazine, the Woodstock Independent, 55 Words, and decomP. Currently, he is putting the finishing touches on his novel and a sitcom pilot, and is the events and marketing coordinator at Read Between the Lynes Bookstore on the square in Woodstock, Illinois.

Chicago: Big City Blinkin'

ELIZABETH BIDWELL GOETZ

I moved to Illinois from California for college, and something was different about it from the get-go. This was noticeable even when visiting schools, back when such a move was still purely hypothetical, back when I thought I'd never be able to live anywhere without an ocean. In the Chicago suburb of Evanston, my parents and I strolled from the campus to the movie theater, passing yuppie boutiques, overpriced chain franchises, and restaurants, just like in Los Angeles. But there were student apartments on the same blocks as preppy coffee joints and weird little drugstores—sometimes even in the same buildings—and old settled houses around the corner. This was new to me, since, in LA, retail and residential areas were separated; the lat-

51

ter may as well have been kept behind gates. And just like those kids in *American Graffiti*, my friends and I depended on cars whenever we wanted to do something other than wander the streets our parents had chosen to live on.

But Evanston, legitimate as claims of its exclusivity may otherwise be, had none of this. You could accidentally end up anywhere in the town, because no matter what you wanted, it was liable to be mixed in with old Victorian houses, frat kids in alleys, or secondhand stores selling yellow-framed sunglasses from the seventies, all entirely irrelevant to your search. However, while the denizens of Evanston had cafes and Chinese takeout pulling them to the most unlikely ends of their suburb, this phenomenon also allowed them the dangerous option of living a life independent of the squalling city immediately south of it.

I ended up moving to Chicago, though, and it was even more thrillingly different from LA. There were El trains! And you could travel the whole city, no slave to any car. I started college in Hyde Park, on the south side of Chicago, but I spent a summer working and subletting an apartment back up in Evanston, and riding the El trains southbound into the city was the best.

I was reading a lot of F. Scott Fitzgerald that summer, spending a lot of time trying to piece together what his characters thought about their relationships to their Midwestern origins. I'd try to figure out how these relationships with the places they were from could be productively applied to my own life. The El was there for me, facilitating everything I needed on its own version of the schedule printed by the Transit Authority, like a flaky friend you have to stand by because he's all too patient a listener when you do get a hold of him.

The Red Line in Chicago curls after it passes Armitage Avenue, where it doesn't deign to stop, before it slows at North and Clybourn. And just there, a few short blocks from where the train heads west during an otherwise southbound trip, is my favorite part of mass transit in all Chicago. Until the Red Line heads due south again at State Street, you can stare out the windows and see Chicago's most beautiful towers. There's the Prudential, the Hancock Center, the Sears Tower, the Wrigley Building, the Tribune Tower, the Carbide and Carbon Building, and the one that looks like an oversized concrete corncob on the river. You can feel those buildings waving to the clouds, staunchly swallowing the caution others may throw to the winds, beckoning college students lost in the summertime, all while the train propels you through that ghetto of Olympian art deco and steel frames that most people just think of as the Loop.

Chicago has always been welcoming. Carl Sandburg's "City of the Big Shoulders" turns out to have arms long enough to hold all its inhabitants tight. The September before my last year of college, I was back in town after six months away. I had spent the spring studying overseas and the summer working a job on the East Coast and staying with distant family friends. By then I knew that Chicago was more my home than California, which, some years, I only visited over Christmas. I could tell this for sure because when I was feeling nervous about job prospects or concerned that I hadn't found an apartment for my return to the States, I found myself picturing my long-ago bedroom back in Chicago. Not that I've lived in places much nicer since, but my room back then was about a hundred square feet of industrial carpet surrounded by off-white concrete walls. Other than a view of an intersection and a fire station, and the most artsy posters and torn magazine pages I could find to cover the walls, it didn't have much going for it. But I realized that I was repeatedly imagining that extra-long twin bed when I needed to think of somewhere calm, the way my horoscope-reading grandmother might suggest that a stressed-out person think of the ocean. But no, no ocean will do it for me. Only a bed from which I can hear cars zooming down numbered city streets, otherwise empty for the night, while I watch the blinking lights of sirens howling across my walls, can send me to sleep these days.

My mother had flown out to Chicago with me that fall to help me cart my boxes out of storage and move them into my new apartment. We arrived late at night, and I can remember the drive in our rented car from Midway Airport to Hyde Park so well. All I did was watch the street signs. We'd opted for surface streets over highways, since this made the car ride a straight shot, and my mother was trying to hold a conversation as she sorted her thoughts aloud. "And then I'll check into the hotel. And in the morning, we'll have breakfast, and I'll see your new apartment, and we'll pick up the bed. Don't forget to call the girl who's selling it to you, okay?" There wasn't much I could have said to expedite her thinking, but I would have been worthless in that department anyway. "Western!" I read off a cross-street's sign. "Street of my youth!" Not that I'd aged much during my time away, but the eras of your life can seem pretty short and specific when you're only twenty-one. "Ashland! I'm so nostalgic!" We were nearing Hyde Park. "The Green Line stop! Look—there's Harold's Chicken! I've spent so many nights waiting for the bus there." I rattled on for my overly patient mother, but I wasn't in any shape to finish a story, because then there was "King Drive! Ellis! Greenwood! University!"

"Elizabeth," my mother said, her voice as terse as it gets. "You're getting a little tiresome."

"I'm sorry," I professed, but I wasn't, not really. These street names were doing incredible things to me. I was back where I belonged. It didn't matter that the intersection of Fifty-fifth Street and Western Avenue was a fairly rough part of town. In fact, most of our drive was through a crime-ridden area where I'd never spent much time, aside from bus rides to the airport. But this was my terrain, even if only from behind the passenger windows of buses and, in this unusual case, my mother's rented sedan.

And then we finally pulled into the garage of the Ramada where my mom had booked a room. I gobbled down carry-out pasta with her as fast as I could, be-cause all I really wanted was to see my friends, people who would understand how important it was to be back in this particular city. But I called my roommate's cell phone and found out that he was with a few of our friends at the Falcon, the best kind of neighborhood bar. The Falcon was about as dark as the summer night outside its doors, the kind of bar with a standoffish personality. It tended to host a primarily middle-aged, African-American crowd, but for this reason, it held a reputation of edgy cool among students who thought they were over the bars closer to campus where they were likely to see their course TAs and their exes alike. Soon after that night, the Falcon rebelled against its role as a refuge of such student rebels, and block-print signs now hang prominently in the windows, claiming to admit "ABSOLUTELY NO PATRONS UNDER THE AGE OF 25."

When it's warm out in Chicago, everyone has to go outside. In February, forty degrees counts as warm and everyone walks around aimlessly, but later in the year, standards adjust a bit, and we only feel forced outside when it's sixty and unlikely to rain. As a result, no one gets anything done in the summer. In Hyde Park, old-fashioned romantic norms manifest themselves. You can learn when friends have surreptitiously started dating, because you'll run into them sauntering along the lakefront hand in hand.

It was still hot when I first returned to town for school that fall. It was so consumingly hot, we'd take breaks from moving furniture into the apartment just to collapse on the cool kitchen floor. But the nights were lovely, warm like they'd never let you go. A couple nights after that hurrah at the Falcon, my friend Sarah and I realized that, now that one a.m. had struck, the temperature had finally sunk low enough that a wander outside was mandatory. We retrieved our flip-flops from the mess on her apartment floor and clambered down her fire escape. We ambled down Fifty-third Street to the lake because, as everyone knows, that's really the only place worth going after eight p.m. in these parts.

The lake is Lake Michigan, the only one we've got. Other neighborhoods have canals or a branch of the Chicago River stopping up their streets with cul-de-sacs. And it's true that we've got a lagoon in Washington Park to the west, frequented mostly by geese and old men sitting on park benches who cheer me on or ask me the time on days my running route takes me their

ing the path that circles the Point, the way everyone does. On the north side of the Point, you can see the tall, tall buildings downtown. It's "the big city blinkin'," just like in that Wilco song, "I Am Trying to Break Your Heart," which my friends and I are convinced is actually set in Chicago. (Wilco's from Chicago, so this makes total sense.) Due east from the limestone blocks, there is only horizon. I swear that once I saw all the way across the lake to its shores in Michigan and Indiana, but that was during the day, and in the spring, too. That night in September, all we could see in that direction was the oil barge that perpetually sits in the water just close enough to the shore that a good swimmer could surely reach it with a bit of effort. Walking clockwise, we came to the southern face of the Point, where the water always seems a little calmer, as if it can feel more at ease because it doesn't have to compete with any famous architecture on that side, just a few neglected piers and the dunes and smokestacks of Indiana.

We scrambled down the stair-step limestone slabs to the sandy beach below, then slid off our flip-flops and stuck our feet in the water, tentatively. The lake had been warming up all summer long, and this was as warm as it got, so we had to go in. We backed up a bit so we could peel off our jeans and dump them on drier sand, and then waded in as far as we dared. Then we headed back to our pants and our shoes, and sat in the sand for a long time.

It's fairly easy to find out who your best friends were when you were little. You only have to look through old photographs and find out who splashed about next to you in wading pools and bathtubs. While I wouldn't want to call companionable descent into the lake's usually freezing waters the only litmus test for friendship, it is certainly true that, at one point or another, I have taken nighttime walks to the lake with all the main characters of my life. Geography in Chicago is weird this way. It has merged with the social. You can narrow down the geographical origins of transplants to Chicago by how they react to the lake—people who have moved there from the west coast have a hard time orienting themselves when the referential body of water is unexpectedly on the east side of everything. And while we have no hills, views of the city are startlingly plentiful; because the streets are straight like the spokes of a bike, you can see the Sears Tower from almost anywhere. And you can often climb the roofs of friends' apartment buildings, or lean over the rails of the bridges that cross back and forth over the river or the Dan Ryan Expressway, to stare out at the city from some new angle. And I think it's this sort of staring up at the big city blinkin' that makes me feel like I really belong to Chicago.

• • •

Elizabeth Bidwell Goetz was born in Santa Monica, California, but has spent most of the past five years in Chicago. She earned her undergraduate degree in English Language and Literature from the University of Chicago in 2008. She pulls the occasional shift behind the registers of the Seminary Co-op Bookstore, where her favorite season is textbook rush.

INDIANA

STATE MOTTO "The Crossroads of America"

STATE SONG "On the Banks of the Wabash, Far Away" by Paul Dresser

STATE FLOWER Peony

STATE TREE Tulip tree

STATE BIRD Cardinal

STATE BEVERAGE Water

STATE INSECT Say's firefly

STATE STONE Salem limestone

RESIDENTS Indianans or Hoosiers

STATE TRIVIA:

• The Empire State Building, the Pentagon, the U.S. Treasury, and fourteen state capitols around the nation are built from Indiana limestone.

• The first successful goldfish farm was opened in Martinsville, Indiana in 1899.

• Santa Claus, Indiana receives over one half million letters and requests at Christmas time.

• Famous Indianans: Michael Jackson, James Hoffa, Dan Quayle, David Letterman, Cole Porter, Shelly Long, Kurt Vonnegut, Jr., Wilbur Wright, Red Skelton, James Dean

Contrary Indiana

RANDY SMITH

For most people, it's pretty easy to answer the question, "Where are you from?" We Hoosiers don't have it quite so easy.

I must first explain the word "hoosier." It probably wasn't intended as a complimentary term in the early days, but Hoosiers today embrace it. The eminent poet James Whitcomb Riley tells us that *hoosier* was a relatively common but now-forgotten term for a laborer, and specifically for workers from Indiana who helped build the navigation canals on the Ohio. According to author Alan McPherson, his Tennessee relatives think it's synonymous with "lazy rustic." Other explanations are too far-fetched to recount here.

I'm often tempted to say I'm from "Barely, Indiana." Three brothers from New York, the Scribners, laid out my city, New Albany, across the Ohio River from Kentucky in the Indiana territory in 1813. Three years later, the territory was granted statehood.

When I moved from Florida to New Albany, I was fortunate in that I quickly met all the "history nuts." My native curiosity ensured that any stranger with a nugget of information about my newly adopted state would be able to unburden himself to an eager student. The first and strongest lesson, though, required the teller to explain a) why Indiana was different from other states and b) why the river cities were unlike the rest of Indiana. It is Barely Indiana, after all, and a majority of Hoosiers seem to think that's just fine.

Our landscape is very different from the rest of the state. Indiana was pretty much scraped flat by glaciers in the last ice age, but there are two exceptions. Up north on Lake Michigan, enormous dunes of sand rise high above the water, providing Hoosiers with a great place for summer getaways. In the south, what the glaciers left behind were the scrapings. We call them "knobs." Here, a mountain-raised boy like myself can pretend he's home. In fact, anyone from West Virginia or East Tennessee, where I was raised, would call them bumps.

A visitor from the Rockies would hardly notice them. But we like them for what they are, even if the commanding view across the Ohio River is of Kentucky.

The love-hate relationship between Indiana and Kentucky is legendary, and we residents of southern Indiana are the front line in that sometimes romance, sometimes feud. Outsiders think it's about basketball (the rivalry between IU and the UK Wildcats is also legendary), but there's more to it than that.

General George Rogers Clark, a Revolutionary War hero, when offered his choice of any of the land under the jurisdiction of the United States as a reward for his service, elected to take his grant of land in the budding Northwest Territory. That is, in Indiana, though Kentuckians continue to claim he actually settled in Louisville. The folks in next-door *Clarks*ville beg to differ. The troops that Clark rewarded with their own grants of land were among the first in a long line of Americans who saw the future in Indiana. They've been leaving Kentucky ever since. Even Abe Lincoln (well, his pa) decided Indiana was the place to be.

As time passed and the white settlers began to eradicate or otherwise displace the natives, Southern Indiana became the jumping off point for new generations of Hoosiers. As the center of gravity moved northward, most of the state forgot where it all started. Even today, when Indianapolis media say "southern Indiana," they're referring to folks on the northern side of the knobs. Heck, for most of the past fifty years, we didn't even share a time zone with the rest of the state, which is pretty peculiar if you've ever seen a map of Indiana. When I moved here, the county courthouse clocks were all set to Indianapolis time, so as to conform to laws made in the state capital. My neighbors even had a term for it: Indy was on "slow time."

Our politics, too, diverge from those of the rest of the state. In 2008, while Indiana turned to the Democratic candidate for president for the first time since the sixties, the people in our environs, nominally Democrats, turned red and rejected Barack Obama. Since Tippecanoe, Indiana has been one of the most reliable Republican states. And for most of that time, Hoosiers in the south were yellow-dog Democrats.

During the War Between the States, the divide became dangerous. Many around here were called "Copperheads," with the implication that they held sympathies for the Confederate cause. In fact, Copperheads were the most extreme of the "Peace Democrats," who wanted nothing to do with the war and thought if the South wanted to secede—let 'em. In gracious thanks, Colonel John Hunt Morgan led the 2nd Kentucky Cavalry Regiment north to raid the cities, towns, and farms of southern Indiana. The Confederates made him General Morgan, and Hoosiers erected historical markers where some farmer lost a cow to the Rebels.

While there were doubtless many sympathizers and appeasers in Southern Indiana, there were many who risked their lives to assist escaping slaves in the years preceding the conflict. New Albany was a significant transit point in the Underground Railroad, a fact that is memorialized in the form of a permanent, award-winning exhibit at the city's Carnegie Center for Art and History.

You can't talk about Indiana without mentioning William Henry Harrison, the soldier who commanded the campaign against Tecumseh, who fought to unite the northern and southern American Indian tribes and halt the advance of white men once and for all. While Andrew Jackson controlled the southern tribes, Harrison gets credit for defeating the northern tribes. Like Jackson, "Old Tippecanoe" also rode his fame to the White House. Unlike Jackson, who served two full terms, Harrison holds the distinction of occupying the nation's highest office for the shortest period. The oldest president except for Reagan, he died just thirty-two days after his inauguration. Unstated within our borders is the fact that Harrison moved to Ohio after settling things in the territory. But then again, his grandson Benjamin gained the presidency decades afterward, and no one disputes that he was a Hoosier.

Indiana can claim a fine sports heritage. Few haven't heard of Bobby Knight, the demanding former coach of the IU basketball team. John Wooden, the UCLA coaching legend, was born and first gained stardom in Indiana. A skinny kid from tiny French Lick also played some decent basketball—Larry Bird. And all those legendary Notre Dame football legends? They lived and played on Indiana soil, in South Bend, in the far north of the state. We are, of course, famous for the Indianapolis Motor Speedway and its featured race, the Indianapolis 500. Nowadays, the Brickyard 400 NASCAR race draws at least as much attention. I've never seen either one. But the most famous of sporting events is the Indiana state high school basketball tournament, which most people say was ruined a few years ago when the schools were sorted by enrollment into multiple classes.

I must acquiesce to that most traditional element of any published state profile, the list of famous Hoosiers. Other than my wife, Col. Virgil I. "Gus" Grissom is my favorite Hoosier. I cried in January of 1967 when he and his Apollo 1 crew died on the launch pad at the then Cape Kennedy. And I cried again when I first got the chance to visit the memorial outside his hometown of Mitchell, Indiana, where at Spring Mill State Park I saw his actual Gemini mission capsule, the Molly Brown. I'll recite a few important literary lights Indiana claims: Theodore Dreiser, Kurt Vonnegut Jr., Booth Tarkington, Gene Stratton-Porter, Rex Stout, Jessamyn West, and Lew Wallace. The fine arts (Twyla Tharp, Robert Indiana); entertainment (David Letterman, Woody Harrelson); or science (Wilbur Wright, Edwin Hubble).

Since 2004, I've made Indiana my home. It was a necessary relocation (I really wanted to sleep in the same bed as my new wife) and a fortuitous one. Moving here, I found my place in life. The bookstore I had always dreamed of became a reality.

And being a curious and cantankerous sort, I asked a lot of questions. Why, I asked, does Indiana do things differently? I'm still learning. It's a peculiar state, and after five years here, I'm willing to say it's filled with good people. We have our own oddballs and kooks and crooks and saints.

And now, I guess I'm one of them. I'm a Hoosier.

P.S. Here's how odd things are here. Our bookstore colleagues in Louisville, Kentucky, the metropolitan city only about two hundred yards south of where I sit, belong to the Great Lakes Independent Booksellers Association. Until a few months ago, we were members of the Southern Independent Booksellers Alliance. Neither of us knows whether we're Southern or Midwestern. Somebody has to fit into the cracks. Guess that's us.

• • •

Randy Smith is the owner of Destinations Booksellers, in New Albany, Indiana. In his spare time, he runs a small publishing operation under the name Flood Crest Press. He was born in Florida, raised in Tennessee, and now calls Indiana home. He has visited all of the forty eight states that were in existence when he was born; in his mind, Alaska and Hawaii are still on probation.

Indiana Basketball Jones

TERRY WHITTAKER

When people think of Indiana, basketball comes first to the minds of many. I, like most of my friends growing up in the late fifties and early sixties, had a basketball goal hanging on my garage, and later, when I was looking to buy a home, a basketball goal was one of the amenities I insisted on.

When I was seven or eight I spent hours trying to get the ball into the basket, but I was too small and weak to get it over the rim. Most of my time was spent either chasing the ball as it caromed off the backboard and down the driveway to the street, or picking up my glasses after the ball clanged off the rim into my face. I often had an audience for these futile attempts, much to my humiliation. I still recall the first time I actually made a basket; I looked around to see if anyone else had witnessed this miracle, but of course there was no one there.

When I got older and taller, my brother, friends and I would play well past sunset on summer nights, shooting into the shadows since there was only a single spotlight at the corner of the house. Three on three was the maximum due to the width of the driveway. This diminutive space led us to develop some incredible trick shots from behind the garage, over shrubs and from great distances since the driveway was over a hundred feet long. Of course these skills never translated into any real basketball talent.

My father, who played for Elkhart High School in the early thirties, taught me the game. He played before the jump shot, so early on I copied his peculiar two-handed set shot. He would plant his feet, move his tongue to the left side of his mouth, begin chewing on it, flex his left knee, raise that leg, push it forward, and then release the ball from high up on his chest. I dropped the tongue chew early on, but found the extended leg kept defenders away. That was important since I was the smallest boy in my class until my senior year in high school.

My friends were endlessly amused by my father's shooting routine, much to his displeasure. After their snickering came a lecture about how none of us would have been able to play for his coach, a demanding but fair man who my father worshipped. If they stuck around long enough they heard comparisons to General George Patton, whom my father fought under in World War II. We were assured Patton would have turned us into the men my father doubted we would become.

My father was a good enough player that he, along with the other starting guard on his team, received a scholarship offer from a small Ohio liberal arts college. My father could not accept since he had to find work immediately after graduation. His friend did, though, and became a teacher and later dean at the school, leaving my father to always wonder what might have been.

(Many years later, I told my father that Bobby Plump, who scored the winning basket for tiny Milan High School in the 1954 state championship, was coming to my bookstore to sign his autobiography. "Plump couldn't hold my jock strap," was my father's half-joking reply. For Christmas that year I gave him a signed copy of Plump's book with the inscription, "Bob, it would be an honor to carry your jock strap.")

Elkhart High School basketball was played in the 8,300-seat Northside gymnasium, which was built in 1954 and was for some time the largest high school gym in the country. The gym was filled on game nights. There was nothing to compare the scale of this gymnasium to in my town of 35,000. We had a three-story department store, but this place, in the eyes of a nine year-old boy, was a temple. It was more awe inspiring than my church, but was also teeming with danger.

I would take the long walk up the collapsible bleachers staring at the gaps in the floor boards. Though I never recall it happening, the space seemed perfect for a small boy to slide through to the floor below, where his tangled body would land amid the cups, wrappers, and articles of clothing which had fallen through. This was a place I knew well, as after most games, I gathered there with other children and adults searching for their hats and gloves. Staring up, the supports seemed far too flimsy for the mass of bodies seated above. I tried not to look too closely at what seemed like structural imperfections. I could hear the thumping of thousands of feet pounding down the stairs and tried to ignore the swaying of the bleachers. I would frantically search for my hat all the while thinking how ironic it would be if I had escaped falling through the floor board only to be crushed when the bleachers collapsed.

High above, near the ceiling, catwalks seemed to levitate without any obvious support. I spent many anxious moments waiting for someone to tumble to the floor below while they navigated these walks like trapeze artists. Hopefully they would not land on our mascot, Blue Blazer, a painted wooden character sitting on a lightning bolt, which looked like an irradiated mosquito from an old B horror movie. It had a menacing scowl, and its corkscrew nose seemed perfect for impaling an unlucky cheerleader who came too near it in a tumbling routine. Many of our opponents had more cuddly mascots, and they would set them next to our Blazer at mid-court before the game. There was something disquieting about seeing a cute stuffed Scottie (Shipshewana-Scott) positioned near the business end of the lightning bolt.

Adding to the menace of the place was my father's behavior at the games. He became someone I hardly knew, screaming and booing. It was never much fun for him just to cheer on the home team; he had to find some coach or player on the opposing team to vilify. He would vent to us, "That number 12 should be thrown out." I was never able to discern what it was the player was doing, but after the game my father would enlighten me. "Dirty player" or "too cocky" were the most common sins. "Didn't you see the way he ran down the floor after he scored; didn't you see the look on his face? Don't let me ever catch you being cocky." Given my size and current lack of any real talent, I didn't see this as a realistic problem.

There was one referee in particular who drew his ire. "Not Dubus again," he would moan as he read the names of the game officials. I think he secretly loved seeing Dubus listed. My dad had the uncanny ability to see traveling and three-second lane violations despite our great distance from the floor. "He's walking," he would scream punching me on the shoulder, "Did you see that?" I never did, but of course nodded my head. "Dubus you bum, are you blind?" he would scream igniting boos of solidarity from those around him. I feared they would turn into a mob storming the floor and stuffing the whistle and the pea inside it (which apparently was not working) down Dubus' throat.

There was something especially disquieting about seeing the mothers of my friends and neighbors acting in this manner. Many of the fathers I had seen being boorish, but the mothers? It was like seeing June Cleaver in full froth. You could see the young kids looking up in disbelief thinking, "Who is this woman and could she turn on me like this?" Thankfully, my mother was not one who displayed this Jekyll-and-Hyde personality.

My father's sensitivity to traveling violations was also on display when he watched games on television. The worst offender in his eyes was Celtic guard Bob Cousy. "He travels every time he touches the ball, and because he's a star the refs let him get away with it," Dad would fume. One time, Cousy was at the free throw line and I said to my father, "Look, Cousy is touching the ball and he's not traveling." "No one likes a smartass," was my father's reply.

My basketball experience was not all dark and fearful. Particularly entertaining were the opposing teams, especially at sectional time, when we played the small county schools. We had over a thousand students in my freshman class alone, and most of the county schools had a couple hundred total. One year Concord, one of the small schools, entered the sectional undefeated. They were undersized and had to play an Elkhart team that had two 6'7" players. One of their small guards tried to counteract this by doing something I had never seen before or since. When one of the tall Blazers was shooting a free throw, he would stand directly behind him at the top of the free throw circle and crouch down to make himself even smaller. When the Elkhart player turned to run down the floor after his foul shot he ran him over and a foul was called. This worked twice, and although at the time I thought it was deceitful, I now think it was pretty inventive. The Concord Minutemen still lost the game.

There were many great high school team names in our area. My favorites were the Jimtown Jimmies, Logansport Berries, Hobart Brickies, La Porte Slicers, Plymouth Pilgrims, and Mishawaka Cavemen. It was a shame that we were too far away to play the Martinsville Artesians, Vincennes Alices, Delphi Oracles, Rising Sun Shiners, Shoals Jug Rox, or the Frankfort Hot Dogs. Some newer schools have joined my list: the River Forest Ingots, Pendleton Heights Arabians, Speedway Spark Plugs, Indianapolis Northwest Space Pioneers and Madison-Grant Argyll Warriors.

Indiana high school basketball is not the same today. With all of life's other distractions, attendance is down significantly from my era, but still, what's better than a hoop in the driveway and an afternoon—or evening—spent bouncing a ball, launching it up into the air? And hey, a swish. What a great sound.

• • •

Terry Whittaker is owner with his wife, Susan, of Viewpoint Books in Columbus, Indiana, which is entering its 37th year in business. After more than fifty years playing basketball he still cannot go to his right.

MICHIGAN

STATE NICKNAME   Wolverine State, Great Lakes State

STATE MOTTO   Si quaeris peninsulam amoenam circumspice (Latin: "If you seek a pleasant peninsula, look about you")

STATE FLOWER   Apple blossom

STATE TREE   White pine

STATE BIRD   Robin

STATE FISH   Brook trout

STATE REPTILE   Painted turtle

STATE STONE   Petoskey stone

STATE TRIVIA:

• Wolverines, gone from Michigan from two hundred years, may have returned.

• No point in Michigan is farther than eighty-five miles from one of the Great Lakes.

• Possibly the first soda pop, Vernor's Ginger Ale, was produced in Detroit.

• Michigan was the first state to guarantee every child the right to tax-paid high school education.

• Famous Michiganians: Tim Allen, William Boeing, Sr., Anita Baker, Francis Ford Coppola, Gerald Ford, Henry Ford, Earvin "Magic" Johnson, Casey Kasem, Charles Lindbergh, Madonna, Dick Martin, Ted Nugent, Iggy Pop, Diana Ross, Bob Seger, Steven Seagal, Gilda Radner, Lily Tomlin, Robin Williams, Stevie Wonder

Michigan Left

JUSTIN WADLAND

MICHIGAN

I have always been coming or going from Michigan, rarely giving it the attention it deserves. My family moved around a lot when I was growing up, staying two years in South Carolina and seven in Vermont, but all my years spent in the Great Lakes State add up to the longest I have lived anywhere. When I wasn't there, I longed for it, and when I returned, I often couldn't wait to leave.

1. MICHIGAN LEFT

Grass-covered medians divide many of Michigan's multi-lane arterials. When you get to an intersection, you will see perplexing signs forbidding left-hand turns. If you want to turn left, you may curse and wonder, *What am I supposed to do?* Don't worry. Soon enough, a lane will conveniently appear on the left side of the road, where you can move over, cross the median, and make a U-turn. Then, going back the opposite way, you will be able to make your right turn. Congratulations! You have executed your first Michigan left.

This feature of Michigan roads was developed in the Sixties so that left-hand turns wouldn't slow the efficient flow of traffic. It can be found all over the state, even in the Upper Peninsula. I passed through these turns innumerable times without knowing their name or purpose, but when I learned about the Michigan left (from an Alaskan, no less), I had found words to describe something essential about Michigan.

2. MICHIGAN RIGHT

"Michigan did not develop a type," reports the 1941 Works Projects Administration guide to Michigan. In other words, you can't easily recognize Michiganders. I know of at least one sure way: As if about to take an oath, we hold up our right hands to mimic the mitten shape of Michigan's larger Lower Peninsula and then point with our left index fingers to where we're from. When I first started college in Kalamazoo, we all stood around locating hometowns on fingers, thumbs, and palms, and among us was an African. He held up his hand, pointed to a space in front of his left hip, and said, "I'm from here."

3. ANOTHER MICHIGANDER LEFT

Of my grandparents' generation, only one or two ventured out of the comfortable hold of Michigan. Of my parents' generation, half of their siblings settled out of state. Of my generation, none (cousins included) stayed in Michigan. Every one of my high school friends left and most of my college friends did, too. Although Michigan remains the eighth-largest state, with a population of just over 10 million, it's losing people. Since 2007, the state's population declined by more than 76,000. When I look at the satellite view of Michigan in Google Maps, I see a gigantic mottled green hand framed in blue water, and it's waving goodbye.

4. PERSONAL GEOGRAPHY
4.1 DETROIT

You can still buy a T-shirt that says, "I'm so Bad I Vacation in DETROIT." My dad had one because we regularly visited his parents in Redford, a suburb outside the city but within the metro area that sprawls like an oversized callus just below the thumb knuckle of Michigan. When I drive through the city, my eyes drift from the road to the gas stations, liquor store signs, church steeples, and house gables that look older than their years. Downtown, shining towers of glass and steel dominate the skyline, but down below molder the magnificent ruins of derelict buildings, like Michigan Central Station with its hundreds of smashed out windows as blank as eye sockets in a skull.

Detroit roads have heavy, substantial names—Inkster, Livernois, Woodward, Middlebelt—that match the heavy, substantial American automobiles they carry. The white population of Detroit took these roads out of the city during the "white flight" that began after World War II and reached full force in the fifties and sixties. My grandparents were among those who left. In a city that had over 1.8 million people in 1950, less than 900,000 remain. The writer Rebecca Solnit recently observed, "Just about a third of Detroit, some forty square miles, has evolved past decrepitude into vacancy and prairie—an urban void nearly the size of San Francisco."

I was born in this city, waiting to leave. My dad had just finished medical school in Ann Arbor, and weeks after I was born we all moved to South Carolina so he could begin his residency.

4.2 LAKE LEELANAU

We moved back to Michigan when I was two, to Lake Leelanau, a town in northern Michigan. Located on a peninsula that juts like Michigan's pinky finger between Lake Michigan and Grand Traverse Bay, the small town shares its name with a nearby lake that is actually two bodies of water connected by a stream. Shining examples of Michigan's 11,000 inland lakes, North and South Lake Leelanau have calm, clear water and sandy shores. I learned how to swim here, and with mask and snorkel I'd submerge to follow snail trails.

We lived in a green house on a pine-covered hill. In spring, we'd search for the pale bone-colored spires of morel mushrooms poking out of the damp leaves. Our black Standard Poodle once disappeared between the ferns and tree trunks and returned with his mouth full of porcupine quills. Winter brought massive snow piles, four times my size and perfect for snow forts. A little over twenty miles away were the Sleeping Bear Dunes, but not until my legs were much longer did I brave the 110-foot slope that looks like a tidal wave of sand.

We moved away from Lake Leelanau when I was five, around the time I was learning to read. Leaving behind the natural wonders of the north, I acquired a taste at an early age for the bittersweetness of nostalgia. I wanted to stay where the wild things are.

4.3 ST. CLAIR

For the next five years we lived on the thumb joint of Michigan, in St. Clair. From the boardwalk downtown, you can watch Great Lakes freighters plow through the azure of the St. Clair River. In summer, teenagers leap from the guardrails, float on the current to the rusted handles of a ladder, and climb out. My eighty-five-year-old grandmother, who learned to swim in the river when she was five and has gone for a dip at least once every year since, occasionally joins the young swimmers. One time a girl said to her, "In twenty years I hope I look as good as you do!" The gap was more than sixty years, but to a kid, twenty years is a lifetime. "If you look like me in twenty years, you're not going to be doing too well," my grandmother told the girl. They both laughed as they treaded water and drifted down river.

The boardwalk is but one example of St. Clair's small town take on urban renewal. Beginning in 1969, the St. Clair Progress Corporation led an effort to refurbish downtown, demolishing the old buildings that once crouched along River Road like remnants of another era. In their place the Riverview Plaza, an outdoor mall, was built. I visited my first bookstore there, a cramped little shop where I bought the 1984 *Guinness Book of World Records* and *Choose Your Own Adventure* novels. Nearby was Groff's Drugstore, where I refreshed my supply of *MAD* magazines. The last time I visited St. Clair, both of these stores and many others had gone out of business. Despite their good intentions, the community leaders couldn't halt the tide of shoppers headed toward the new malls outside of town. My family moved from

St. Clair to Vermont when I was ten, and perhaps this is why I gaze past the FOR RENT signs in the windows and instead fill up the vacant space with my good memories.

4.4 OKEMOS

Before my senior year of high school, we moved right back into the palm of Michigan when my dad took a job at Michigan State University medical school. After the green mountains of Vermont, Michigan looked bland and ugly. Despite my persistent frown, my new classmates were friendly enough to invite me to hang out. We sometimes went to a pizza place that had a black-and-white photo of the town's namesake, Chief Okemos, hanging on the wall. He was an old man with a cane and gray hair covered by fabric wrapped like a turban around his head. The scowl on his face contrasted with the little blurb that portrayed him as a lovable, drunken Indian who frequented the porches of white settlers. He looked sad and grumpy to me, and I wondered what he would think of the suburbs and industrial parks, shopping plazas and parking lots, Olive Gardens and Home Depots that now occupy his wilderness.

One place near the mall offered some solace: Schuler Books, a large, independent bookstore. Inside the squat, rectangular brick building, I easily forgot my angst toward the urban sprawl just outside. I bought everything I could by Kurt Vonnegut and built my collection of Jack Kerouac, William Burroughs, Henry Miller, Charles Bukowski, and other authors that fit my adolescent taste for literary bad boys. I remember once standing between the shelves, wishing that I could telepathically absorb everything contained within the pages around me. I wanted all the texts to shine like beams of light into me, conveying their knowledge and wisdom. I did not know it at the time, but I would dedicate my life to carrying out this vision, and I fully blame the town of Okemos for driving me to it.

4.5 KALAMAZOO

I spent seven long, confused months attending Kalamazoo College, located on the left side of the heel of Michigan's hand. The small liberal arts school—now over a hundred and fifty years old—attracted me because its chapel on a hill and old brick buildings looked a lot like the East Coast schools I couldn't get into. Just off campus, though, Michigan returned in all its glory. A short walk away was the Burger King where Elvis was sighted alive and well in 1988. "He's not heavy anymore," Louise Wellings told reporters at the time. My friends and I frequented this establishment, and I kept my eyes peeled. The prospect of sighting Elvis always added a dash of excitement to the Whoppers I scarfed down.

4.6 EAST LANSING

If Michigan has what palm readers call a life line arcing from just above the thumb down to the base of the hand, then the Michigan State University campus sits right on the apex of it. When I transferred there, I gladly disappeared into the masses of 40,000 students that double the population of East Lansing each academic year. MSU was the first land-grant institution in the country dedicated to teaching scientific agriculture, and according to the WPA guide, "All students were required to labor several hours a day to clear campus." By the time I attended, the university sometimes called "Moo U" was ranked nationally among the top party schools.

I spent my first couple of years sampling what

MSU had to offer in the way of social gatherings, drifting through the crowded frat parties, the backyard and basement keggers, and the raucous celebrations or bitter lamentations after sports events. I was not a good Spartan, though; I never went to games, never learned the fight song, never took my stand in the eternal rivalry with the University of Michigan.

Out of boredom, I sought out the nooks of Pinball Pete's, which had enough pinball machines to devour an evening's worth of quarters, and the crannies of the MSU Library, the first research library I ever used. This huge rectangular chunk of brick and glass contained so many shelves of books that I had to rely on signs that listed call number ranges next to pieces of brightly colored tape. Looking down, I'd find the corresponding trail of orange, chartreuse, or some other shade leading off into the stacks. In this way, I was gently guided into the labyrinth toward authors like Mikhail Bulgakov and Italo Calvino and topics like the Hells Angels and Voodoo. Somewhere I got lost and still haven't found a way out.

4.7 PICTURED ROCKS

Like most Michiganders from the Lower Peninsula,

I only visited the Upper Peninsula on vacation. The mysterious land across the Mackinac Bridge is inhabited by a rare breed of Michigander referred to as the "Yooper" (U.P.'ers), who talk a lot like Canadians and live in the least populated area of the state. The year I graduated from college, I hiked for four days along Pictured Rocks, sandstone cliffs that rise a hundred feet or more above Lake Superior. I was reading Gary Snyder at the time, and as the days passed, I began to feel like I had stepped inside one of his poems. My friends and I followed a rolling trail along the shoreline, and when we got too hot, we ditched our packs and dove into Superior. Beneath the swells, the white sandy bottom was visible, before dropping into crystalline depths. Above, the cliffs displayed striations of rust, dun, and rose.

Later, I lay on my stomach in one of the many shallow streams flowing out of the forest toward the lake. The cool water pressed on my shoulders and tugged on my legs, swirling particles of sand over my fingers. I finally understood what Snyder meant:

> droplets regather
> seek the lowest,
> and keep going down

in gravelly beds.
There is no use, the water cycle tumbles round—

This Michigan stream had flowed into Lake Superior for innumerable seasons, and I briefly shared its grace. When I returned home to East Lansing, I had trouble translating what I had seen into my everyday life. Dissatisfied with my prospects in Michigan, I soon took the roads that lead out of state.

5. MICHIGAN RETURN

When we lived in Vermont, we would often drive through upstate New York and Ontario to get to Michigan and cross over the Blue Water Bridge at Sarnia. When I was eleven or twelve, I sat in the front seat of our Ford Econoline van as we climbed the bridge toward Port Huron. Out my window, beyond the girders whipping by, the shimmering expanse of Lake Huron stretched to the horizon, meeting a sky filled with cumulus clouds. But then I began looking forward. We had been driving for twelve hours, my butt was sore, and ahead was a land shaped like a hand cradling so many of my friends and family. I was so eager to get there, I began pressing the soles of my feet with all my might against the floor mat. "I'm the first person in Michigan!" I declared as we passed beneath the sign welcoming us to the Great Lakes State, and we began to descend toward the place I am from.

• • •

Justin Wadland is a librarian at the University of Washington, Tacoma Library. For the past three years, he has been a regular reviewer of documentary films for *Video Librarian*. As a participant in the MFA program in Creative Writing at Pacific Lutheran University, he is writing a collection of nonfiction stories about the anarchist colony in Home, Washington.

Tough Enough Michigan

BILL CUSUMANO

S now provided my initiation to Michigan and was partially the reason why I eventually become a resident. I had spent my first two years of college at Wake Forest and discovered that my philosophy radically differed from that of the Southern Baptist Convention. Also, I definitely was not comfortable in a society still permeated by Jim Crow. Deciding to transfer, I was accepted by both Michigan and Wisconsin, and in March of 1968, I traveled to visit the schools.

Flying into Detroit, I was greeted by a mild snowstorm and received small doses of the white stuff all three days I was in Ann Arbor. Having left the balmy clime of North Carolina, I was not a happy camper as I moved on to Madison. Only Wisconsin had more

101

snow—a lot more. I immediately made one of those intelligent decisions for which nineteen-year-olds are justifiably famous and decided to attend Michigan.

Author and screenwriter Lowell Cauffiel tells prospective writers, "never start with the weather." I have already violated his first rule but I would venture to guess Mr. Cauffiel, a Michigan native, has more than once mounted his motorcycle on a pristine morning only to be caught in a deluge later that day.

I suspect he would forgive me; weather is such a dominant factor of life in Michigan. The climate can be extreme and varied, often in the same day. Michigan is home to tornadoes, blizzards, massive thunderstorms, high winds—almost anything except hurricanes—and if you live here, you learn to be prepared. During the winter there are at least two pairs of shoes in my office, and I'm not unique. Only a fool would venture out on a Michigan morning without wearing boots. It is not uncommon to see people carrying umbrellas on a sunny day, as storms can rise quickly. Sandbags and cement bags can be found in the trunks of cars in winter for extra weight and traction on snowy, icy roads, and balaclavas, wool caps, quilted coats, and padded gloves are items of necessity. Michigan's economy may be in the depths at the moment, but its residents certainly do a good job of maintaining the profits of clothing manufacturers.

Such weather is caused by the element that defines Michigan and gave the state its name—water. The name comes from a Native American word meaning "big water," and *big* may not even be the proper adjective. Michigan is enclosed on three sides by four of the five Great Lakes, creating the state's two distinct peninsulas.

Numbers can barely convey the magnitude of the Great Lakes, but think about just a few. The shoreline of Michigan covers 3,200 miles; only Alaska has more. The lakes contain 20% of the earth's fresh water, and, if they were to magically drain would inundate the continental United States to a depth of ten feet. Actually, the term *lake* is a misnomer for any of the five giants. *Inland sea* might be far more appropriate. They are massive on a scale that cannot be discerned from a map.

I had my first view of Lake Michigan in 1972. My boss at the time had a summer cottage on its shore and I drove across the state one weekend for a visit. Michigan is mostly flat land, having been scraped clean by glaciers eons ago, so I was shocked when I approached a gentle rise, crossed it, and was confronted with an endless expanse of water. Having grown up on the east coast, I was used to limitless vistas of water, but that was the Atlantic Ocean. Never had I expected such a view from a lake.

Their size can even create strange illusions. There have been reports of shipwreck survivors suffering from dehydration; being stranded in the midst of one of the giants presents the aspects of an ocean, and people forget that they are floating in fresh water.

The lakes certainly can mirror oceans in the manner of their storms. Gordon Lightfoot made famous the gales of November on Lake Superior, and the depths provide a treasure trove for divers descending upon the numerous wrecks. I once watched a storm over Lake Huron. The water was churning, crashing, and putting on a demonstration of power that was worthy of the Atlantic or Pacific.

All that water has been nature's highway. It served the native inhabitants and provided a route for the first Europeans and all who followed. Today the freighters still ply the lakes but recreational boating dominates, as Michigan ranks in the top three for boat registration.

But the proliferation of water does not end with the four titans. The landscape of Michigan is dotted with lakes (more than Minnesota, in fact), rivers, streams, and ponds. Water is so prevalent that it is impossible to go more than twenty miles in any direction and not encounter it.

Just as it is hard to understand the size of the Great Lakes, most people do not realize how much space Michigan covers geographically. When John Smolens wrote his novel, *Cold*, we had success selling it in our store in Ann Arbor. A representative of his publisher noted this and called to ask if John could drive over some day and sign books. I had to gently inform her that Mr. Smolens was over 450 miles away in Marquette and it would not be a leisurely commute.

There are towns in the Upper Peninsula located 650 miles from Detroit, and before modern highways, a trip between the two was a major expedition. During the late sixties and early seventies, while the Selective Service Act was still in force, all draft physicals for the state of Michigan were conducted at old Fort Wayne on the Detroit riverfront. Those residents from the UP had to endure bus trips of fourteen hours or more to enjoy the prodding of Army doctors. While going through the stations, potential inductees could also observe a great anomaly of Michigan geography: at any moment, a person could look out a window and see Canada due south across the river.

No state has a population that is homogenous, certainly not one that encompasses the distances of Michigan. But even with huge urban areas like Detroit and vast empty spaces like the Upper Peninsula, the people of Michigan tend to have one thing in common: a strong independent streak.

Perhaps it arises from the early days when Michigan was, literally and figuratively, a wild frontier, or perhaps it comes from having to confront the erratic climate, or maybe it is from the varied immigrant strains searching for freedom, but Michiganders are not prone to conformity. This is a state where William Milliken, a Republican department store owner from Traverse City, served as governor for fourteen years while Democrat Phil Hart, a man so liberal that if he were in office today he could drive Rush Limbaugh to new heights of vitriol, was in the Senate. Such ticket splitting is not uncommon and cannot be explained solely by the concept of urban versus rural.

There may be no correlation, but I have always felt this independent attitude was the cause for an amazing aspect of Michigan's people, which is a great generosity, both in spirit and substance. Drop into the Ann Arbor Moose Lodge on any afternoon following work and you will discover the regulars seated at the bar. These men are mechanics, electricians, bus drivers. They are passionate fans of University of Michigan football, even though none ever attended a class there. This is NASCAR country. They voted for George Bush and constantly berate the intellectuals who dominate city government. Tax is the foulest word in their lexicon, and many firmly believe the income tax is unconstitutional. And they all give tremendously of their time, labor, and money to any cause they consider worthwhile.

Charity is not uncommon in Michigan, and across the state, charitable donations per capita have consistently been above the national average. During the holiday season of 2008, with the Michigan economy mired and layoffs at near-record levels, the Warm the Children campaign in Washtenaw and Livingston counties clothed over 3,900 children—a record. The same result occurred in the Adopt a Santa program in Ann Arbor; across the state similar stories were reported. This kind of giving is a mindset, and you have to believe its roots lie in the fact that this is the epitome of a blue-collar state. The people of Michigan understand hardship and deprivation, knowing very well that dangers lurk for everyone.

There is a sculpture in Detroit of a fist, a huge fist. It stands outside Joe Louis Arena to commemorate the man who held the longest-ever heavyweight boxing title. It is a stark, simple, and powerful image that perfectly conveys the force and strength embodied in Louis. But it could just as easily be a symbol for the entire state. Michigan was built on hard, enervating, yet enduring labor. Men chopped trees, dug copper, trapped for fur, and fished the rivers and lakes.

Finally, of course, that labor reached its peak in Detroit as Henry Ford and the Dodge brothers and their contemporaries created the mighty auto industry. Today, the car manufacturers are held in low esteem, but there is no denying that they revolutionized American society. And that revolution was built by the hands of workers in their factories.

If the fist can symbolize the raw strength of Michigan labor, another piece of art gives it its humanity. Travel up Woodward Avenue from the Detroit River and the Arena, and in the Detroit Institute of the Arts behold Diego Rivera's magnificent murals portraying the workers of Ford's River Rouge Plant, once the world's largest factory. The production line has been portrayed as dehumanizing, but Rivera gave it a face and the laborers became individuals. It was these people—and those in other industries—who not only built the cars but the very middle class that became the backbone and substance of the American Dream. The Ford family even epitomized the generosity of spirit found in Michigan when they commissioned the well-known Communist artist to produce the murals, ignoring the contradiction between their politics. The Rockefellers, in a similar situation, rejected Rivera.

Of course, Michigan is not a Shangri-La of toleration. Henry Ford was possibly the country's leading anti-Semite, and the Detroit riot of 1967 is seared in the national consciousness. It was not the first. Many blacks had come north in the 1930s to escape the oppression of the South and the migration escalated during World War II when the Detroit plants retooled and became the Arsenal of Democracy. The influx of black workers, along with poor Southern whites and entrenched residents, raised racial tension and conflict that resulted in a riot on Detroit's Belle Isle in 1943.

Yet this is also a state that has a proud history with the Underground Railroad, and many slaves passed through Michigan on the way to Canada. In my county, I can visit sixteen sites associated with the Railroad. It is also a place where Governor G. Mennen Williams refused to extradite one of the infamous Scottsboro Boys, who had escaped prison and, following history's path, sought refuge in Michigan.

The Michigan of today is better than that of 1967, but it is certainly not perfect. Maybe the election of Barack Obama proves America is starting to accommodate itself better to the racial divide, but Detroit and its suburbs still battle, and the undercurrent is tinged more by black and white than outskirts and city. Such remnants of old prejudice are frustrating, but hope always remains because of that core at the center of Michigan's population, that generosity, that basic goodness—that Midwestern politeness, if you will. Michiganders know good fences make good neighbors but also know it is a better fence if they help each other to build it.

The individual spirit also engenders respect, and there is nothing the people applaud more than those who work. A blue-collar ethic prevails in Michigan at all levels. Just look at the professional sports teams. They are all in Detroit but really represent the whole state. "Going to Work" was the motto of The Pistons' last NBA championship, and the 2006 Tigers run to the World Series was driven by the mantra "Nine Innings." Leave it to Michigan to love millionaire athletes for putting in a full day of labor.

As I write I can look out the window and see snow. I have no more love for it now than I did forty years ago, but I have learned to adapt. I am, obviously, a Michigander. Winter is something to be endured, a penance to be paid for all there is to be enjoyed. I love the water and boating on the lakes. I love the museums and music clubs of Detroit. I love the titanic expanse of Sleeping Bear Dunes overlooking Lake Michigan. I love the long summer days that for so long allowed me to indulge my passion for softball well into the night. Most of all, I love the people, confounding as they (like all people) may be at times. They are staunch, honest, loyal without pretense. They share a common ground and usually do it with uncommon grace.

Go back a few years to a chilly, rainy night in June. The Tigers are in the middle of a disastrous season, but on this night Comerica Park is abuzz. The Los Angeles Dodgers have come to Detroit for the first time in interleague play. Scattered throughout the stands and concourse are black men wearing Brooklyn Dodgers replica jerseys with the number 42, honoring Jackie Robinson. Most of these men never had the opportunity to see him play but have come out tonight in respect because his team is here. The percentage of African-Americans in Detroit is one of the highest in American cities, and the name Jack Roosevelt Robinson carries greater esteem here than in most places. In the bottom of the ninth, the Tigers are losing again and the Dodgers bring in the unbeatable Eric Gagne to save the victory.

So, what do these old black men, and all of us, do? We pump our fists in the air in unison with the rest of the crowd, exhorting the Tigers to rally. Of course, they do. They live in Detroit. They live in Michigan.

• • •

Bill Cusumano is the head buyer at Nicola's Books in Ann Arbor, and he is descended from the great Sicilian winemaking family.

OHIO

STATE MOTTO   "With God all things are possible"

STATE SONG   "Beautiful Ohio"

STATE TREE   Ohio buckeye

STATE BIRD   Cardinal

STATE ANIMAL   White-tailed deer

STATE BEVERAGE   Tomato juice

STATE INSECT   Ladybug

STATE GEM   Ohio flint

RESIDENTS   Ohioans

STATE TRIVIA:

• The Cincinnati Red Stockings became the first professional baseball team in 1869.

• In 1914 the first traffic light in America was installed in Cleveland, Ohio.

• Akron, Ohio was the first city in the country to have police cars.

• Oberlin College, in Oberlin, Ohio, was the first college in the U.S. to accept women.

• Ohio comes from the Iroquoian word meaning "great river."

Small Town, Big Heart Ohio

LIZ MURPHY

T here is *something* about Ohio.

Ignore all you've heard about the terrible winters and the gray days. I've lived all over the country, enjoyed the majesty of the Pacific Ocean, the balmy breezes of the Eastern Shore, the old majesty of Georgia, and the hard red clay of Oklahoma. It's the people that make Ohio the best place to live.

After moving across the country twelve times in eleven years, I settled in northeast Ohio thirty years ago—and fell in love. Our town is a little bit of New England transported to the Middle West. 210 years ago, Hudson, Ohio was founded by David Hudson, a settler from Connecticut, and if you remove the traffic and the satellite dishes, you could almost believe you are still in that era. While we have our share of corporate movers who come in for a few years and leave, Hudson has a core of people who love it and love its heritage. Several hundred homes and buildings have been awarded historic plaques and the owners have maintained the buildings' historic integrity. We are about to have the 60th Annual Home & Garden Tour, and after all these years in town, and thanks to a husband who "handily" built a major addition and a mother who left me the legacy of a fabulous garden, both my home and garden are featured this year. This is preceded by the annual Ice Cream Social on the Village Green.

The Hudson Clocktower graces the northwest corner of the Green, right across the street from the historic Main Street shops. Many of these shops, including my bookstore, The Learned Owl Book Shop, have been on Main Street for decades. The Grey Colt (ladies' fashions) is celebrating fifty years and is owned by the founder's daughter.

If I walk into Hudson's Restaurant, they automatically bring me a diet Coke if it's breakfast time, or pour a glass of Chardonnay with ice if it's 5 p.m. (At lunch, they have to ask!) If I'm walking down the street and see a sweater I have to have in a window, I can take it with me and call the store later with my credit card number.

Hudson has carefully preserved a lot of land in the center of town, all referred to as greens. They are well used. Every year on Mother's Day Saturday, the Boy Scouts sell hanging baskets and flats of plants on the South Green. There are Summer Sunday concerts in the bandstand on the Gazebo Green, and Friday Night concerts on the First & Main Green. Summer brings a Farmers' Market every Saturday to the Village Green, and you see families pouring in and out from all directions with their recyclable grocery bags. We have the annual Wine Festival, Taste of Hudson Festival, and Art on the Green, and many people walk to all these events. It's a walking town, with a good portion of the residents within walking distance of downtown and the greens.

When I was growing up in Maryland, turning twelve was a huge birthday, because my biggest present was the certificate that granted me permission to "Cross the Boulevard" and venture even farther from home by myself. Hudson, Ohio, is the kind of town where kids can still come to shop on their own, once they are old enough to cross a major street. Parents and kids know that any shopkeeper is a good guy and will be a safe haven in an emergency. Hudson is a town where most people leave at age eighteen to go to college, but we are having an influx of young families in their thirties returning to raise their children.

I know my neighbors in Hudson, knew them from the day I moved in, because they came over to welcome me. (I lived in southern California for eight months and didn't even know my neighbors by sight, thanks to eight-foot-tall privacy fences). We pick up one another's papers and mail, have keys to each other's houses, and supply food and wine for each other in emergencies (and sometimes non-emergencies).

While some people dread the snow, I love a good blizzard. Last winter we had people skiing down Main Street to visit some of the shops, and I snow-shoed to work one day with my dog. (Yes, we have a shop dog, one of several in town, and there used to be shop cats in several stores. Ruby, our third Bookshop Dog, has a great many fans of all ages).

Hudson has all the wonderful values of heartland America, and most of the advantages of a much larger city. We have an outstanding public school system, a very progressive library, a professional theater, and are home to Western Reserve Academy, a world-renowned prep school. Many Hudsonites are executives at major corporations in Cleveland or Akron. This summer we will have our first Theater Festival (think Shaw Festival forty years ago). Because of all these things, we draw well-known authors, musicians, and speakers to our town.

Chance brought me to Ohio in 1979, but the lovely, caring people caused us to build an addition on our house to make aging-in-place easier, and this lovely town in this fabulous state is where I plan to spend all my remaining days.

• • •

Liz Murphy is the owner of The Learned Owl Book Shop in Hudson, Ohio.

Ohio Nights

DEB COVEY

Crackling fire and a clear, dark sky spotted with thousands of stars. A gathering of cousins ranging in age from two to sixty-two, who have arrived at this place from several corners of the country, various careers and family configurations, to simply enjoy one another's company.

We recounted tales of summer vacations at the lake, perfecting synchronized swimming routines under a cloudless, bright blue sky, while our parents fished, went frog gigging, or fascinated us with their waterskiing talent. The absolute randomness of our childhood days inspired us to ruminate on how busy our own children's summers were, filled with swim teams, soccer games, basketball camps, and gymnastics, and how

121

busy our summers were at work. We swore to ourselves that we wouldn't let this happen to our grandchildren. Our parents worked as well but devoted two weeks every summer to simply playing at the lake. Everyone worked hard, whether they were farmers or industrial giants or educators. Teenage summers were spent working at the Dairy Queen or detasseling corn for DeKalb. Before you could get a work permit you mowed lawns or babysat. Then you played.

Back then, county fairs exploded all over the state with 4-H-ers peddling the cows, pigs, chickens and lambs that they had spent many winter months fattening up. Cities were visited, with many frenzied summer days spent in Cincinnati, Columbus, Dayton and Sandusky.

Summer and fall provided endless entertainment through sports, professional and/or backyard. If you are from Ohio you know who your baseball team is before you are out of diapers.

You are either an Indians or Reds fan and generally speaking your team is supported by your entire family. Similarly you know your football team before you can walk; you are either an Ohio State or a Michigan fan, a Browns or a Bengals fan. Civil conversations with strangers avoid sports more than they do religion or politics.

For some of the cousins the most exciting days were spent at amusement parks—King's Island if you were from mid-to-southern Ohio or Cedar Point if you were from northern Ohio. My feelings toward amusement parks could be compared to the anticipation that a contestant in a survival show would feel before being immersed in a pit of snakes. The excited conversation that my friends had before arriving at the park only provoked images of terror in me. I was a cautious kid and I knew that the roller coaster, the Racer, was going to derail while I was on it.

Ohio is also a great place to just read, and that is where I found my space. Libraries with their old-booky smell, school marm types who whisper *shhh*, cool tile floors and oak tables all excited me. Curling up in my room or outside under a tree was heaven and provided a window into the world. While I grew up in a small community, I never, ever felt distanced from cities like New York or Chicago, London or Tokyo, because I could read about them.

That evening with my cousins I realized that Ohio

was a great place to live and grow because it allowed me the opportunity to work and play and explore, to stretch my limits while still staying connected with my roots.

• • •

Deb Covey is head buyer at Joseph-Beth Booksellers—with stores in Cincinnati and in Cleveland, Pittsburgh, Lexington (Kentucky) and Charlotte (North Carolina)—as well as the Davis-Kidd stores in Tennessee.

My Oh My, O-hi-o

RICHARD HUNT

Ohio. Those lovely vowels, those round letters that roll around in my head, slipping and sliding like marbles. If I were a modern-day Demosthenes, I'd stand not on the seashore (more on this later) but instead high on a bluff overlooking that twisty river that forms our southern border with West Virginia and Kentucky, and there I would lift my voice to the sky and say—"Oh, I love, O-hi-o."

Ohio is a crazy quilt stitched together of farms, factories, and football fields, schools, silos and split-level suburbs. The major cities queue up in alphabetical order: Akron, Bowling Green, Cleveland, Columbus, Cincinnati, Canton, Dayton. Look, how polite and proper. There's also evidence of Western Civ envy here in the

Buckeye State: Troy, Macedonia, Athens, London, Dover, Lebanon, Oxford, Dublin, Toronto, Cambridge, Lima, Xenia. But if this international lust might veer toward a tricky pronunciation, the ever-so-practical Ohio orientation simply opted for famous dead guys: Napoleon, Euclid, or Solon.

We are musical. In the fifties, Ohio rocked-n-rolled when Alan Freed started spinning the platters. Well before the R&R Hall of Fame occupied primo North Coast real estate on Lake Erie, these Ohio bands played sweaty sets and hallelujah encores: Michael Stanley Band, Chrissie Hynde and the Pretenders, Pure Prairie League, Guided by Voices, Joe Walsh and the James Gang, and of course, the Ohio Players. We whipped it with Devo, James Brown, Bootsy Collins, and Macy Gray. We sang along with Tracy Chapman, Over the Rhine, the O'Jays, Robert Lockwood Jr., Eric Carmen, and Dean Martin. Then we shook it all night long with the Afghan Whigs, Pere Ubu, Nine Inch Nails, Marilyn Manson, King Records and the Agora Ballroom. Baby, baby, baby, this is why the buzzards from WMMS rule the airwaves.

There are hay wagons and railroad cars full of almanac data that attempt to define the seventeenth state of the Union. Bushels of corn and soybeans. Tons of salt mined under Lake Erie. At one point in America's development, Ohio rocked. Cincinnati was the sixth largest city in America in 1850 (when the country ran on rivers). Cleveland was the fifth largest city in the United States in 1920 (when the country ran on coal). Ohio was on the front burner of the Industrial Revolution as third-shift steel workers bellied up to the bar at dawn, burping from their breakfast beer while smokestacks belched cinder, sulfur and soot in the background. The Buckeye State grew by dint of backbreaking labor and a stubborn streak two hundred miles wide. We've got mended holes in our clothes, grime that evaded the ten-penny scraped under our nails, and for the most part we sleep well at night because we're stinking exhausted . . . except of course for twice weekly when we stare at the ceiling and worry about foreclosure.

This is not to imply we're all darkly dour stick-in-the-muds. The state seal has a blazing sunrise—an ode to the power of positive thinking. When you get to that lyric in "America the Beautiful" about amber waves of grain—that's Ohio, marking the eastern fringe of the plain, tasseled in cornsilk and wheat. No shining sea, no purple mountain majesty. Just dirt; bountiful, beautiful dirt that tills easy and crumbles just right when you pick it up. Then when you squeeze your hand tight into a fist, it packs like a perfect brown snowball, an earth bomb that would leave a dent if you threw it hard enough. Rich "growing-stuff," topsoil with a physical and metaphoric weight and substance to it.

Having lived in the Big Apple, Southern California and Beantown, I often heard folks claim the "need" to be by the sea. Something about the waves. Now I don't want to speak for all Ohioans, but all the slapping and slurping and tiding up and down makes such a racket. Makes me edgy too—all that restlessness and ceaseless F. Scott Fitzgerald beating against the shore. Unfortunately, scientists tell us we might indeed have an ocean as a neighbor in the near future. For many reasons, here's hoping I don't live to see, nor hear, that.

So why, oh why do we live here? For one thing, because you can *live* here.

I've noticed in my time away that as people tend to crowd up on either edge of the country, they speak of their door-to-door commute as some sort of daily gauntlet. Here in Cin City, I've got a one-song commute. If it's a long song, and I'm not talking Don McLean's "American Pie," I just wait and listen to the end. You can pretty much get anywhere PDQ—on the highway, it's a mile a minute; in town, it's not much longer. So every day (seriously, every day) you can work and exercise, meditate and read, take the kids to school, meet a friend for lunch, mow the lawn, listen to the ballgame, supervise homework, do the dishes, and talk on the phone. On weekends, you can sit in a lawn chair, watch the kids play with the dog, visit the grandparents, go to church, skip church, make a mess and clean it up, and all the above.

Nor is Ohio ever the same. Each day clicks slightly differently as there are four full seasons to pepper the year. The topography—from top to bottom, side to side—varies as well. You just have to pay attention to savor the slight mile-by-mile changes which otherwise would sneak by you. Right after we got evicted from college, a.k.a. graduation, my housemate Tony and I set out to ride the Cardinal Greenway, a bike route that was mapped out by connecting back roads running from Indiana to Pennsylvania. With our front tires pointed toward the morning sun, the physical diversity of the state played out in front of us in super hi-def, clearer and finer than any IMAX movie: a western horizon seemingly a hundred miles away, rolling hills north of the state capital, then one week later, we climbed and cussed into the Appalachians. Even after living two decades in this state, we passed through towns we'd never seen before and talked to folks whose tales we now treasure. Wonder of wonderful wonders.

Still, it would be disingenuous to paint this place as the Midwest Mecca. We've got issues, we've got problems, just like any other place. Still, I'll give you five good reasons why I live in Ohio.

First, we don't take ourselves too seriously. The state flag is a pennant, for heaven's sake. Even though our cities hearken back to classical eras or world explorers, our history is splattered like a farm boy stepping in a cow pie: "The Mistake on the Lake," the Cuyahoga River (which burned); the Mapplethorpe exhibit; Charlie Manson. On Ohio's political front, there's been two hundred years of *faux pas*. Cleveland's mayor couldn't make it to a foreign dignitary dinner because it was his bowling night. Jerry Springer was the mayor of Cincinnati—go figure. For others, the name is enough: Jim Traficant; Dennis "Roswell" Kucinich; Wayne Hayes. And that's the minor leagues. While Ohio may be called the "Mother of Presidents," none of the politicos who made it to the White House distinguished themselves much better than those who stayed at home.

Second, as this is a blue-collar state, we have blue-collar sports and sports teams. Wrestling is big here (and, to go on record, wrestling is the most physically, mentally and spiritually demanding sport on the planet. But I'm not biased.) Not WWF or whatever they call those actors in a ring. No, this is the sport of mat burns and cross-faces, spitting to cut weight, arm bars, fireman's carries, and fierce, fierce, unbending control and calculation. Plus for those who can't take it, there's also football, boxing, basketball, soccer, softball, and lacrosse. Ohio's pro teams? Ouch! Each one somehow at some time snuck in and won a couple championships over the decades and now they all have a chip on their shoulder and a penchant for getting close but falling short. Ernie Byner's fumble on the goal line. John Elway's g—d—toothy grin. Joe Montana's pass to John Taylor in the '89 Super Bowl. Don't bet on Pete Rose. The Indians' ninth-inning chokes. Ohio State's streak of national runner-ups. But we got Shaq now, and he says let's win a ring for King LeBron.

Third, our truly and rightfully famous people have given others light and flight and inspiration: Thomas Edison, Wilbur and Orville Wright, John Glenn, Neal

Armstrong, Jesse Owens, and Gloria Steinem. But we're such a mix of backgrounds, the muggles of the Midwest, so our heroes and heroines are sensible, hardworking, unassuming and caring. They'd rather have a window than a mirror. They'd rather stand than sit. They'd rather play than watch. They'd rather make the soap than orate on a soapbox.

Fourth, Ohio loves books. Makes sense—each of these itty-bitty words (*Ohio* and *books*) has two O's snuggled up tight; coincidence, I think not. For your consideration, here's our literary legacy: Sherwood Anderson, Thomas Berger, Ambrose Bierce, Erma Bombeck, Hart Crane, Rita Dove and Sharon Draper. Paul Laurence Dunbar, Allan Eckert, Harlan Ellison, Nikki Giovanni, Zane Grey, Richard Howard, William Dean Howells, Langston Hughes, John Jakes, Daniel Keyes, William Matthews. Make way for Robert McCloskey, Toni Morrison, Mary Oliver, Dawn Powell, John Crowe Ransom, R. L. Stine. Hail Harriet Beecher Stowe, Mildred Taylor, James Thurber and Roger Zelazny. Ohio loves its bookstores, booksellers, libraries and librarians, and even the wacky publishers. But most of all, Ohio loves readers.

Fifth—and this is all in testament to that which has

on the patio." Thirty minutes later, the route tracked into Cleveland proper, where grimy businesses shouldered up to the sidewalk and the residents hung out on the stoops, and when passing by the West Side Market, the street was slick with hosed-away lettuce, onions and motor oil. Then it was up and over a breath-taking bridge where downtown Cleveland awaited like the Emerald City—shiny skyscrapers, bustling department stores (the real-life set for "A Christmas Story"), one-way streets and men in ties and girls in skirts. My head spun with new writers, new sights, and new longings.

Case #2: cut to today. Our little publishing house, which struggles like every other, nonetheless was given a stake by investors who believe in our goal, believe in books, believe in the spirit of our undertaking and the impact the written word can make in one's life. So they lifted us on to their shoulders not because they saw great piles of gold at the end of the rainbow, but because they cared for us, and more for you and every other reader out there. They listened to our plans and looked us in the eye and said "okay." Of all the people I've met across this great country, and for all the time I spent in the media capitals of New York, Boston, Los Angeles and San Francisco, I don't believe that in any one of those places I would have found folks who care this much about our waking dream to connect authors and readers. They're giving us a chance here, where in other places you have to enter with your head bowed, hand out, and tail between your legs. Local business is not only smart business, it's all about this community and doing right by these fine, fine people.

Case #3: Ohio girls. It's easy to fall in love with Ohio girls, but I'm not so sure it's easy to be an Ohio girl. Think about growing up XX in ornery, knucklehead, banged-up, and bruised Ohio. For the qualified opinion, though, you'd have to ask my sisters, or my wife, or my daughter. But be respectful and get to the point quickly, as they don't suffer fools. This representative group of women is smart, strong and set in their ways, a gang of five whose collective will is as steadfast as a barn beam and whose character is forged like the steel that rolled out of the mills destined for shipyards, auto plants, and skyscrapers. My late mother, never quite five-foot tall and not quite one hundred pounds, walked two miles home in a twenty-degree snowstorm because she didn't want to trouble anyone to use their phone in the homes she passed by en route. In Ohio, strong and smart still counts. Ask Annie Oakley. Ask Belle Sherwin. Ask Victoria Woodhull.

I got lucky. The Ohio beauty I fell for lured me back time and again. Ours was a long-distance wooing, my love described and our lives foretold via letters. And most importantly, when I ran out of words, I gave her my favorite books, which, truth be told, probably carried the day and ultimately did more to win her over than my rambling thoughts that ran across the paper. And now I love our Ohio family beyond words.

So while I might leave this state occasionally for work or to visit friends, I'm always eager to come home. When pressed, I tell others that the only way I'm leaving for good is in a pine box. But here's the truth of it: I'm stuck here and glad for it. Like the unglamorous parsnip, my life is rooted here in Ohio's rich, brown earth. These tendrils not only anchor us, but they feed us, and in turn, make things sweet. At the end of each day, and at the end of each season, we harvest what we've sown. You get back what you've put into it. So flow our days, and our lives, as the native tribes called the Mighty River: O-hi-o.

• • •

Richard Hunt grew up in North Royalton, Ohio, a lonnnnnng time ago. When he moved to New York City, he reassured his mother by saying, "Don't worry. I've got nothing anyone would want to steal: just old albums, old clothes, and books." His second day walking around NYU, he was amazed by the number of people with tables on the sidewalks upon which they sold "used" albums, clothing, and books. Tours of service include time at Bantam Doubleday Dell, Houghton Mifflin, F&W Publications, and now, Keen Communications, home to Clerisy Press, Menasha Ridge Press, and Wilderness Press.

ABFFE

275 Seventh Avenue New York, New York 10001
www.abffe.com 212-587-4025

Sept. 25, 2009

Dear Reader,

Thank you! By purchasing this book, you have contributed to the fight for free speech in the United States. HarperCollins is donating a portion of the proceeds to the American Booksellers Foundation for Free Expression (ABFFE), the bookseller's voice in the fight against censorship.

ABFFE fights censorship legislation at the state and federal levels. It is a leader in the fight to protect the privacy of bookstore records and is currently campaigning to restore the safeguards for reader privacy that were eliminated by the USA Patriot Act. In conjunction with the National Coalition Against Censorship, it sponsors the Kids' Right to Read Project, which opposes the hundreds of challenges to books that occur in schools and libraries every year. ABFFE is a sponsor of Banned Books Week, the only national promotion of the freedom to read.

We appreciate your support!

Sincerely yours,

Chris Finan

Chris Finan
President

THE GREAT LAKES INDEPENDENT BOOKSELLERS ASSOCIATION AND THE MIDWEST INDEPENDENT BOOKSELLERS ASSOCIATION

LIST OF BOOKSELLERS

ILLINOIS

57th St. Books 1301 East 57th St., Chicago, IL 60637
773-684-1300 www.semcoop.booksense.com

Anderson's Bookshop 123 W. Jefferson, Naperville, IL 60540
630-355-2665 www.andersonsbookshop.com

Anderson's Bookshop 5112 Main St, Downers Grove, IL 60515
630-963-2665 www.andersonsbookshop.com

Azizi Books 134 Lincoln Mall Drive, Matteson, IL 60443
708-283-9850 www.azizibooks.com

Barbara's 1100 Lake St. Oak Park, IL 60301
708-848-9140 www.barbarasbookstore.com

Book Bin, Inc. 1151 Church St., Northbrook, IL 60062
847-498-4999 http://bookbin.booksense.com

Book Cellar 4736-38 N. Lincoln Ave., Chicago, IL 60625
773-293-2665 www.bookcellarinc.com

Book Mouse 820 LaSalle St., Ottawa, IL 61350
815-433-7323 www.bookmouse.org

Book Shelf 252 South Side Square, Carlinville, IL 62626
217-854-4040

Book Stall At Chestnut Court   811 Elm St., Winnetka, IL 60093
847-446-8880   www.thebookstall.com

Book World   300 S. Main St., Galena, IL 61036   815-776-1060

BookBundlz   1419 W. Byron St, Chicago, IL 60613   773-726-3509

Books on First   202 W First St., Dixon, IL 61021
815-285-2665   www.booksonfirst.com

The Bookstore, Inc.   475 N. Main St., Glen Ellyn, IL 60137
630-469-2891   www.justthebookstore.com

Café Book   395 Lake St., Antioch, IL 60002
847-395-2223   www.cafebook-antioch.com

Chicago-Main Newsstand   860 Chicago Ave., Evanston, IL 60202
847-425-8900   www.chicagomain.com

Christian Pages   PO Box 957384, Hoffman Estates, IL 60169
800-939-7922   www.christian-pages.com

Great Debate Books   535 Maine #3, Quincy, IL 62301
217-221-9673   www.greatdebatebooks.com

Magic Tree Bookstore   141 North Oak Park Ave., Oak Park, IL 60301
708-848-0770   www.magictreebookstore.com

Read Between the Lynes   129 Van Buren St,. Woodstock, IL 60098
815-206-5967   www.readbetweenthelynes.com

Seminary Co-op   5757 South University Ave., Chicago, IL 60637
773-752-4381   www.semcoop.booksense.com

Sly Fox   123 N Springfield, Virden, IL 62690
217-965-3641
Town House Books   105 N. 2nd Ave., St. Charles, IL 60174
630-584-8600

Women & Children First 5233 North Clark St., Chicago, IL 60640   773-769-9299   www.womenandchildrenfirst.com

INDIANA

Big Hat Books   6510 Cornell Ave., Indianapolis, IN 46219
(317) 202-0203   www.bighatbooks.com

Bookmamas, Inc.   9 Johnson Ave., Indianapolis, IN 46219
317-375-3715   www.bookmamas.com

Bookshelf-Batesville   101 N Walnut St., Batesville, IN 47006
812-934-5800

Bookworm Inc. 114 N. Michigan, City Center, Plymouth, IN, 46563   574-935-9674

Destinations Booksellers
604 East Spring St., New Albany, IN, 47150
812-944-5116   www.destinationsbooksellers.com

Don's Books   815 N Washington St., Kokomo, IN, 46901
765-459-4901   www.hazeltineandgraham.com

Imagination Station   26 East Jefferson St., Franklin, IN, 46131
317-736-9636   www.istationonline.com

Kids Ink Children's Bookstore
5619 North Illinois, Indianapolis, IN 46208
317-255-2598

Mitchell Books   6360 West Jefferson Blvd., Fort Wayne, IN 46804
260-432-2665   www.mitchellbooks.net

MJ's Bookmark   414 S. Main Auburn, IN, 46706
260-925-2330

Mudsock Book & Curiosity Shoppe
11631 N. Fishers Station Drive, Fishers, IN 46037
317-579-9822

Mystery Company 233 2nd Ave. SW, Carmel, IN 46032
317-705-9711 www.themysterycompany.com

Next Page Bookstore & More
208 W. Monroe St., Decatur, IN 46733
260-724-9027 www.nextpagebookstore.com

Page by Page 1801 N Wayne St., Angola, IN 46703
260-665-9841

Reader's World 4027 Franklin St., Michigan City, IN 46360
219-872-1882

Summer's Stories 131 South Main St., Kendalville, IN 46755
260-349-1745 www.summersstories.com

The Wild 884 Logan St., Noblesville, IN 46060
317-773-0920 www.gotothewild.com

Three Sisters Books & Gifts 7 Public Square, Shelbyville, IN 46176
317-392-2270 www.threesistersbooks.com

Viewpoint Books 548 Washington St., Columbus, IN 47201
812-376-0778 www.viewpointbooks.com

Village Lights Bookstore, Inc. 110 East Main St. Madison, IN 47250
812-265-1800 www.villagelightsbooks.com

Von's Book Shop 315 West State St., West Lafayette, IN 47906
765-743-1915

Wabash College Bookstore
301 West Wabash Ave., Crawfordsville, IN 47933
765-361-6095 www.wabash.edu/bookstore

MICHIGAN

2nd Glance Books, LLC
1001 Welch Rd., #110, Commerce Twp, MI 48390
248-960-1030

Another Look Books 22263 Goddard Road, Taylor, MI 48180
734-374-5665

Aria Booksellers 216 West Grand River Howell, MI 48843
517-548-5577 www.ariabooksellers.com

As the Page Turns, LLC
149 N. Center St., Ste 102, Northville, MI, 48167
248-912-0085 www.asthepageturns.biz

Best Books 1204 Jackson Crossing, Jackson, MI 49202
517-780-0024

Bestsellers Bookstore & Coffee Co.
360 S. Jefferson, Mason, MI 48854
517-676-6648 www.bestsellersbookstore.com

Between The Covers
152 East Main Street, Harbor Springs, MI 49740
231-526-6658

Black River Books
330 Kalamazoo Street, Suite 2, South Haven, MI,49090
269-637-7374 www.blackriverbooks.net

Book Beat Ltd. 26010 Greenfield, Oak Park, MI 48237
248-968-1190 www.thebookbeat.com

Book Nook 42 South Monroe Street, Monroe, MI 48161
734-241-2665 www.booknookmonroe.com

Book Nook & Java Shop 8726 Ferry Street, Montague, MI 49437
231-894-5333 www.thebooknookjavashop.com

Book Shoppe   316 N. State Street, Alma, MI 48801
989-463-1667   www.bookshoppe.org

Book World   112 Aurora Street, Ironwood, MI 49938
906-932-5787

Book World   515 Shelden Avenue, Houghton, MI 49931
906-482-8192

Book World   Delta Plaza Mall, Escanaba, MI 49829
906-786-3973   www.bookworldstore.com

Book World 136 W Washington Street, Marquette, MI 49855
906-228-9490

Book World   407 Bridge Street, Charlevoix, MI 49720
231-547-2005

Book World 404 Ashman Street, Sault Suite, Marie, MI 49783
906-632-0559

Book World   52 N. State Street, St. Ignace, MI 49781
906-643-7569

Book World   Midtown Mall, Iron Mountain, MI 49801
906-779-1416

Bookbug   3019 Oakland Drivem, Kalamazoo, MI 49008
269-385-2847   www.bookbugkids.com

Bookman   715 Washington Street, Grand Haven, MI 49417
616-846-3520   www.bookmangrandhaven.com

Books & More   119 N. Superior Street, Albion, MI 49224
517-629-7560   www.forks.org/booksandmore

Books Connection   19043 Middlebelt, Livonia, MI 48152
248-471-4742   booksconnection@ameritech.net

Boyne Country Books   125 Water Street, Boyne City, MI 49712
231-582-3180   www.boynebooks.com

Brilliant Books   305 St Joseph Street, Suttons Bay, MI 49682
231-271-7323   www.brilliant-books.net

Carol's Paperbacks Plus
5947 Highland Road (M59), Waterford, MI 48327
248-674-8179

Cottage Book Shop   5989 Lake Street, Glen Arbor, MI 49636
231-334-4223   www.cottagebooks.com

Cranesbill Books   108 E. Middle Street, Chelsea, MI 48118
734-433-2665   www.cranesbillbooks.com

Crazy Wisdom Bookstore
114 South Main Street, Ann Arbor, MI, 48104
734-665-2757   www.crazywisdom.net

Everybody Reads Books & Stuff
2019 East Michigan Avenue, Lansing, MI 48912
517-346-9900   www.becauseeverybodyreads.com

Fireside Books 1110 W Michigan Ave., Ste C, Marshall, MI 49068
269-781-3800   fireside.books@sbcglobal.net

Fitz's Booknook   114 Newman, East Tawas, MI 48730

Forever Books 312 State Street, St Joseph, MI 49085
269-982-1110   www.foreverbooks.net

Grandpa's Barn 385 Fourth Street, Copper Harbor, MI 49918
906-289-4377

Great Lakes Book & Supply   840 Clark Street, Big Rapids, MI 49307
231-796-1112   www.greatlakesbook.com

Great Northern Bookstore   209 S. State, Oscoda, MI 48750
989-739-7960   www.oscodastomp.com/greatnorthernbookstore

Hidden Room Book Shoppe
518 Phoenix Street, South Haven, MI 49090
877-637-7222

Horizon Books, Inc. 243 East Front Street, Traverse City, MI 49684
231-946-7290   www.horizonbooks.com

Horizon Books, Inc. 317 East Mitchell, Petoskey, MI 49770
231-347-2590   www.horizonbooks.com

Hostetter's News Agency
135 Washington St, Grand Haven, MI 49417
616-842-3920

I.H.S. Christian Books, Gifts & More
36103 Plymouth Road, Livonia, MI 48150-1400
734-422-9998

Island Bookstore 7372 Main Street, Mackinac Island, MI 49757
906-847-6202   www.islandbookstore.com

Island Bookstore & Coffee Shop
215 E. Central Avenue, Mackinaw City, MI 49701
 231-436-2665 www.islandbookstore.com

Kazoo Books 407 N. Clarendon, Kalamazoo, MI 49006
800-516-2665   www.kazoobooks.com

Kazoo Books   II 2413 Parkview, Kalamazoo, MI 49008
269-553-6506   www.kazoobooks.com
Ladels   1413 Brooklyn, Detroit, MI 48226
313-963-8550   www.ladelsbooks.com

Leelanau Books   109 North Main, Leland, MI 49654-0035
231-256-7111   www.leelanaubooks.com

Literary Life Bookstore & More, Inc.
758 Wealthy Street SE, Grand Rapids, MI 49503
616-458-8418   www.literarylifebookstore.com

Little Professor Book Center
105 W. Shiawassee Ave, Fenton, MI 48430
810-513-2393   lpbcfenton.booksense.com

Local Flavor   125 Water Street, Boyne City, MI 49712

Log Mark Bookstore   334 N Main Street, Cheboygan, MI 49721
231-627-6531   www.cheboyganretailers.com/logmark.html

Lowry's Books   22 N. Main Street, Three Rivers, MI 49093-1532
269-273-7323   www.lowrybooks.com

Lowry's Books and More   118 W. Chicago Road, Sturgis, MI 49091
269-651-6817   www.lowrysbooks.com

Marwil Bookstore   4870 Cass Avenue, Detroit, MI 48201-1204
313-832-3078   www.marwilbookstore.com

McLean & Eakin Booksellers
307 E. Lake Street, Petoskey, MI 49770
231-347-1180   www.mcleanandeakin.com

Michigan News Agency   308 W Michigan, Kalamazoo, MI 49007
269-343-5958   www.michigannews.biz

Nicola's Books   2513 Jackson Road, Ann Arbor, MI 48103
734-662-0600   www.nicolasbooks.com

North Shore Books   315 Center Street, North Muskegon, MI 49445
231-981-0606   www.northshorebookstore.com

North Wind Books   601 Quincy Street, Hancock, MI 49930
906-487-7217   www.northwindbooks.com

North Wind Books at Finlandia University
601 Quincy Street, Hancock, MI 49930
906-487-7309   www.northwindbooks.com

Page One Bookstore & Café
7331 Old Mission Drive, Rockford, MI 49341
616-916-5294

Paperback Book Exchange
1811 S. Mission, Mount Pleasant, MI 48858
989-772-5473   home1.gte.net./paperbac

Pooh's Corner   1886 1/2 Breton Road SE, Grand Rapids, MI 49506
616-942-9887   www.poohscornerstore.com

Read It Again Books   39733 Grand River, Novi, MI 48375
248-474-6066

Reading & Rhythm   110 E Huron Avenue, Bad Axe, MI 48413
989-269-6300

Reading Tree   5300 Northland Drive NE, Grand Rapids, MI 49525
616-363-1051   www.readingtreebooks.com

Research Unlimited   4546 Merkel Lane, Oscoda, MI 48750
989-739-3294   www.research-unlimited.com

Rivertown Bookstore   126 E. Bridge Street, Portland, MI 48875
517-647-5743   www.rivertownbookstore.com

Robbins Book List   320 S. Lafayette Street, Greenville, MI 48838
616-754-4354

Round Lake Book Store
107 Mason Avenue, Suite 102, Charlevoix, MI 49720
231-547-2988

Safe Harbor Books   16 E. M-134, Cedarville, MI 49719
906-484-3081   www.safe-harbor-books.com

Saturn Booksellers 133 W Main Street, Gaylord, MI 49735
989-732-8899 www.saturnbooksellers.com

Schuler Books & Music Downtown
40 Fountain St. NW, Grand Rapids, MI 49503
616-459-7750 www.schulerbooks.com

Schuler Books & Music
2660 28th Street SE, Grand Rapids, MI 49512
616-942-2561 www.schulerbooks.com

Schuler Books & Music – Eastwood
2820 Towne Center Blvd. Lansing, MI 48912
517 316 7495 www.schulerbooks.com

Schuler Books & Music – Okemos
1982 Grand River Ave., Okemos, MI 48864
517 349 8840 www.schulerbooks.com

Schuler Books & Music – Alpine
3165 Alpine Avenue, Suite C, Walker, MI 49544
616 647 0999 www.schulerbooks.com

Self Esteem Shop 32839 Woodward, Royal Oak, MI 48073
248-549-9900 www.selfesteemshop.com

Singapore Bank Bookstore 317 Butler Street, Saugatuck, MI 49453
269-857-3785

Snowbound Books 118 N. Third Street, Marquette, MI 49855
906-228-4448 www.snowboundbooks.com

Source Booksellers 4201 Cass Avenue @ Willis, Detroit, MI 48201
313-832-1155

Taylor's Books and More 60 W. Chicago Street, Coldwater, MI 49036
517-278-2340 www.taylorsstationers.com

Third Mind Books   123 N. Ashley, Suite 208, Ann Arbor, MI 48104
734-994-3241 www.thirdmindbooks.com

Tree House Books   37 East 8th Street, Holland, MI 49423
616-494-5085 www.treehousebooks.net

Tuesday Books 137 W. Grand River Avenue, Williamston, MI 48895
517-655-9700 www.tuesdaybooks.com

OHIO

Appletree Books Inc. 12419 Cedar Road, Cleveland Heights, OH 44106
216-791-2665

Ashland Univ Bookstore Hawkins-Conard Student Center, Ashland, OH
44805   419-289-5301 www.ashlandbookstore.com

Athens Book Center, Inc. 74 E. State, Athens, OH 45701
740-592-4865 www.athensbookcenter.net

Beehive Books 25 N. Sandusky Street, Delaware, OH, 43015
740-363-2337 www.beehiveat25.com

Blue Manatee Children's Bookstore 3054 Madison, Cincinnati, OH,
45209
513-731-2665 www.bluemanateebooks.com

Book Shelf, LLC   152 E. Aurora Road, Northfield, OH, 44067
330-468-3736

Books 'N' More   28 W. Main Street Wilmington, OH, 45177
937-383-7323

Books of Aurora   PO Box 305, Aurora, OH, 44202
330-995-3228 booksofaurora.com

Bookshelf   7754 Camargo Road, Cincinnati, OH, 45243
513-271-9140   bookshelf@fuse.net

Cleveland Museum of Natural History Museum Store
1 Wade Oval Drive, Cleveland, OH, 44106
216-231-4600 x3239   www.cmnh.org

Fireside Book Shop   29 N. Franklin Street, Chagrin Falls, OH, 44022
440-247-4050 www.firesidebookshop.com

Florence O. Wilson Bookstore
College of Wooster-Lowry Center, Wooster, OH, 44691
330-263-2421 www.wilsonbookstore.com

Frogtown Books, Inc.   2131 N. Reynolds Road, Toledo, OH 43615
419-531-8101 www.frogtownbooks.com

Fundamentals   25 W. Winter Street, Delaware, OH 43015
740-363-0290 www.funbooksandmore.com

Jay & Mary's Book Center
1201-C Experiment Farm Road, Troy, OH 45373
937-335-1167 www.jayandmarysbooks.com

Joseph-Beth Booksellers Rockwood Pavillion
2692 Madison Road, Cincinnati OH 45208
513-731-7770 www.josephbeth.com

Joseph-Beth Booksellers Legacy Village
24519 Cedar Road, Lyndhurst, OH 44124
216-691-7000 www.josephbeth.com

Kenyon College Bookstore   106 Gaskin Ave., Gambier, OH 43022
740-427-5710 www.kenyon.edu/bookstore.xml

Learned Owl Book Shop   204 North Main, Hudson, OH 44236
330-653-2252   www.learnedowl.com

Mack Bookstore & Office Supply
1373 Stone Drive, Harrison, OH 45030
513-367-7243

Mac's Backs Books on Coventry
1820 Coventry Road, Cleveland Heights, OH 44118
216-321-2665 www.macsbacks.com

Mind Fair Books   13 W. College Street, Oberlin, OH 44074
440-774-6463

Nanna's Bookstore   26597 N. Dixie Hwy, Perrysburg, OH 43551
419-873-0030 www.nannasbookstore.com

National Underground Railroad Freedom Center
50 East Freedom Way, Cincinnati, OH 45202
513-333-7738   www.freedomcentergiftshop.org

News-Readers Inc.   4 W. Main St., Fairborn, OH 45324
937-879-4444

Ole' Book Nook 1637 E. Rt 36, Urbana, OH 43078
937-652-1531

Page By Page—The Bookstore
840 S Main Street, Bowling Green, OH 43402
419-354-2402

Paragraphs Bookstore
105 S Main Street, Mount Vernon, OH 43050-3418
740-392-9290   www.paragraphsbookstore.com

Stately Raven Bookstore
1315 North Main Street, Findlay, OH 45840
419-427-2814   www.statelyravenbookstore.com

Sugden Book Store 282 Front Street, Marietta, OH 45750
740-373-0347   sugden@ee.net

Trinity Commons Books & Gifts
2242 Euclid Avenue, Cleveland, OH, 44115
216-774-0470   www.trinitycommonsbooks.com

Village Bookworm 435 N. Whitewoman Street, Coshocton, OH 43812
740-623-6564

Wooster Book Company
205 West Liberty Street, Wooster, OH 44691
330-262-1688   www.woosterbook.com

WISCONSIN

A Room of One's Own 307 W Johnson Street, Madison, WI 53703
608-257-7888   www.roomofonesown.com

Apple Blossom Books LLC 513 N. Main Street, Oshkosh, WI 54901
920-230-3395   www.appleblossombooks.com

Back to Books 520 Second Street, Hudson, WI 54016
715-381-1188   www.backtobooksonline.com

Book Heads 216 E. Mill Street, Plymouth, WI 53073
920-892-6657   www.bookheadstore.com

Book Look 2724 Post Road, Stevens Point, WI 54481
715-341-2665

Book World 52 N. State Street, St. Ignace, MI 49781
906-643-7569

Book World 30 N. Third Avenue, Sturgeon Bay, WI 54235
920-854-4248

Book World 10580 Country Walk Drive #11, Sister Bay, WI 54234
906-854-4248

Book World 134 S. Main Street, Shawno, WI 54166
715-524-3837

Book World 10553 Main Street, Hayward, WI 54843
715-634-6007

Book World   121 N. Main Street, Waupaca, WI 54981
715-256-9393

Book World   211 W. North Water Street, New London, WI 54961
920-982-5267

Book World   85 S. Main Street, Fond du Lac, WI 54935
906-922-2980

Book World   1136 Main Street, Stevens Point, WI 54481
715-344-5311

Book World   1723 Main Street, Marinette, WI 54143
715-735-5188

Book World   907 S. 8th Street, Manitowoc, WI 54220
906-682-9202

Book World   320 Watson Street, Ripon, WI 54971
920-748-7680

Book World   414 S. Central Avenue, Marshfield, WI 54449
715-387-6667

Book World   Taylor Heights, Sheboygan, WI 53081
920-694-0011

Book World   58 N. Brown Street, Rhinelander, WI 54501
715-369-2627

Book World   116 Front Street, Beaver Dam, WI 53916
920-887-8711

Book World   522 Oneida Street, Minocqua, WI 54548
715-356-7071

Book World   725 – Fifth Avenue, Antigo, WI 54409
715-623-2500

Book World   114 E. Wall Street, Eagle River, WI 54521
715-479-7094

Book World   253 W. Grand Avenue, Wisconsin Rapids, WI 54495
715-421-2570

Book World   317 Broadway, Wisconsin Dells, WI 53965
608-254-2425

Book World   135 – Third Street, Baraboo, WI 53913
608-356-5155

Book World   105 N. Main Street, Rice Lake, WI 54868
715-234-8038

Book World   120 W. Cook Street, Portage, WI 53901
608-742-1989

Book World   300 E. Main Street, Watertown, WI 53094

Book World   921 E. Main Street, Merrill, WI 54452
715-539-9557

Book World   301 W. Main Street, Ashland, WI 54806
715-685-9998

Bookends on Main, LLC
214 E. Main Street, Menomonie, WI 54751
715-233-6252

Bookfinders   1001A Brilowski Road, Stevens Point, WI 54482
715-341-8300

Bookland   224 W. Wisconsin Avenue, Neenah, WI 54956
920-725-6550

Books & Company   1039 Summit Avenue, Oconomowoc, WI 53066
262-567-0106   www.booksco.com

Boswell Book Company 2559 N Downer Ave, Milwaukee, WI 53211
414-332-1181 www.boswellbooks.com

Bramble Bookstore 117 S. Main Street, Viroqua, WI 54665
608-637-8717 www.bramblebookstore.com

Brown Street Books 25 S. Brown Street, Rhinelander, WI 54501
715-362-5111

Butterfly Books 118 N. Broadway, DePere, Wi 54115
920-339-1133 www.butterflybooks.com

Camelot Corner Books 303 Winneconne Avenue, Neenah, WI 54956

Chequamegon Book Co. 2 E. Bayfield Street, Washburn, WI 54891
715-373-2899 www.abe.com/home/cheqbookco

Conkey's Book Store 226 E. College Avenue, Appleton, WI 54911
920-735-6223 www.conkeys.com

Cover to Cover Books & Gifts
202 Wisconsin Avenue, Tomahawk, WI 54487
715-453-0727 www.cover2coverbooks.com

Creekside Books
W62 N596 Washington Avenue, Cedarburg, WI 53012
262-546-0004

Dragonwings Bookstore 108 N. Main Street, Waupaca, WI 54981
715-256-9186 www.dragonwings.com

Fireside Books and Gifts
1331 W Paradise Drive, West Bend, WI 53095
262-334-1444

HelpWithCancer.org 137 Red Fox Trail, St. Croix Falls, WI 54024
715-271-5037 www.helpwithcancer.org

IslandTime Books & More
1885 Detroit Harbor Road, Washington Island, WI 54246
920-847-2565 www.islandtimebooks.com

Jabberwocky 711C Highway 45 N, Eagle River, WI 54521
715-479-4425   cynthiawith1@aol.com

Janke Book Store 505 3rd Street, Wausau, WI 54403
715-845-9648 www.jankebookstore.com

LaDeDa Books & Beans, Inc.
1624 New York Avenue, Manitowoc, WI 54220
920-682-7040 www.ladedabooks.com

The Little Read Book 7603 W State Street, Wauwatosa, WI 53213
414-774-2665   www.littlereadbook.com

MHS Bookstore   Memorial High School, Eau Claire, WI 54701
715-852-6301

Next Chapter Bookshop
10976 N Port Washington Road, Mequon, WI 53092
262-241-6220   www.nextchapterbookshop.com

Northwind Book & Fiber
205 Walnut Street, Spooner, WI 54801
715-635-6811   www.northwindbook.com

Novel Ideas
8085 Highway 57, Baileys Harbor, WI 54202
920-839-1300   www.novelideas-books.com

Ocooch Books & Libations LLC
145 W Court Street, Richland Center, WI 53581
608-647-8826 www.ocoochbooks.com

Pages & Pipes 322 W College Avenue, Appleton, WI 54911
920-734-2821

Pages & Pipes 748 W Northland Avenue, Appleton, WI 54914
920-830-0309

Paper Tiger Book Store 100-D City Center, Oshkosh, WI 54901
920-231-0800

Pastimes PO Box 396, Princeton, WI 54968   920-295-4801

The Prairie Bookshop
117 E Main Street, Mount Horeb, WI 53572
608-437-4118

Rainbow Bookstore Cooperative
426 W Gilman Street, Madison, WI 53703
608-257-6050   www.rainbowbookstore.org

The Reader's Loft
2069 Central Court, Suite 44, Green Bay, WI 54311
920-406-0200   www.readersloftbookstore.com

Redbery Books, Inc.
43455 Kavanaugh Road, Cable, WI 54821
715-798-5014   www.redberybooks.com

Thyme Worn Treasures 30 N Main Street, Rice Lake, WI 54868
715-736-0233

The Velveteen Rabbit Bookshop & Guest House
20 E Sherman Avenue, Fort Atkinson, WI 53538
920-568-9940 www.velveteenrabbitbookshop.com

UWM Bookstore
2200 E Kenwood Boulevard, Milwaukee, WI 53211
414-229-4201   www.bookstore.uwm.edu

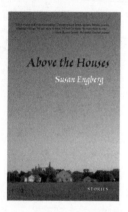 

The Pig Did It

a novel by Joseph Caldwell

"The macabre comedy plays out in sparkling dialogue, with some hilarious speeches that are both incantations of Irish mythology and masterful bits of parody."
—*Washington Post Book World*

"Caldwell's Irish pig is my new love. Caldwell has achieved the impossible with poetic ascents to the peaks of hilarious prose. You will laugh your arse off." —**Malachy McCourt**

PAPERBACK • $13.99

Freshwater Boys

stories by Adam Schuitema

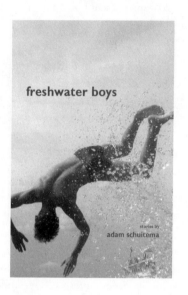

Each of these stories, most of them set in the author's own Dutch-American community in and around New Era, Michigan, pits people against nature, whether the contrast involves someone trying to build a pathetic beach in "Sand Thieves," or a man nearly being killed by snow and ice when he goes for a run in the story "The Lake Effect."

COMING IN MARCH 2010

MALE OF THE SPECIES, stories by Alex Mindt

"In this remarkable debut, Alex Mindt skillfully portrays a series of unique and compelling worlds. The result is a captivating collection that is a joy to read." **—John Searles**

Clowns, deadbeats, refugees, social climbers all bound by the mysterious ties of fatherhood. Alex Mindt's debut collection is like a chorus of fathers and those they love singing in many accents of the paternal connection that befuddles, enobles, enrages and endures. Each unique voice rings true and clear according to its character.

MERCY, by Alissa York

A gifted Canadian writer makes her debut in the United States with a dark and spellbinding tale of forbidden love.

"York's unflinching but tender eye for the natural world results in graceful ballets of description: butchering techniques have seldom been described in such precise, loving detail, and the flora and fauna of the bog are invested with vibrant individuality."
—Publishers Weekly

VIRGINIA LOVERS, by Michael Parker

In the autumn of 1975, a small town struggles with the mysterious murder of Brandon Pierce, a gay teenager found dead in his parents' bed following a high-school keg party. As Thomas Edgecombe, the editor of the town's newspaper, diligently reports on the crime, he begins to suspect that his two sons may know more about the murder than they're letting on.

Welcome to the

Literary Midwest

A Booklover's Paradise!

From the Heartland, this indispensable guide to great bookstores, libraries, and coffeehouses, historic author homes, and famous settings details the best of the Midwest.

You can retrace the path of writers and their beloved characters. Walk down the actual Main Street that novelist Sinclair Lewis described in his most famous novel. Visit Laura Ingalls Wilder's *Little House on the Prairie*. Get lost in the same cave that Tom Sawyer and Huck Finn regularly explored. Listen in on the tall tales in the Burlington, Wisconsin annual Liars' Club contest. Travel in the footsteps of Ernest Hemingway, who spent many summers with his family in Michigan, commemorated in his Nick Adams stories.

You'll also find many of the first preservationists here, including novelist Wallace Stegner and Aldo Leopold, author of *A Sand County Almanac* and the father of the modern environmental movement. Other poets and writers offer visits to sand dune architecture, the expanse of the prairie, the breadth of the sky.

The
BOOKLOVER'S
GUIDE
to the
MIDWEST
A LITERARY TOUR

GREG HOLDEN

Best of all, there's a guide to everyone's favorite bookstore, here in the middle of the U.S.A. Come join the fun—visit the Land of Booklovers!